Make Way for the Spirit

The Blumhardt Source Series

Christian T. Collins Winn and Charles E. Moore, editors

Make Way for the Spirit

My Father's Battle and Mine

CHRISTOPH FRIEDRICH BLUMHARDT

Edited by Wolfgang J. Bittner
Translated by Ruth Rhenius, Simeon Zahl, Miriam Mathis, and
Christian T. Collins Winn

PLOUGH PUBLISHING HOUSE

Published by Plough Publishing House
Walden, New York
Robertsbridge, England
Elsmore, Australia
www.plough.com

Plough produces books, a quarterly magazine, and Plough.com to encourage people and help them put their faith into action. We believe Jesus can transform the world and that his teachings and example apply to all aspects of life. At the same time, we seek common ground with all people regardless of their creed.

Plough is the publishing house of the Bruderhof, an international community of families and singles seeking to follow Jesus together. Members of the Bruderhof are committed to a way of radical discipleship in the spirit of the Sermon on the Mount. Inspired by the first church in Jerusalem (Acts 2 and 4), they renounce private property and share everything in common in a life of nonviolence, justice, and service to neighbors near and far. To learn more about the Bruderhof's faith, history, and daily life, see Bruderhof.com. (Views expressed by Plough authors are their own and do not necessarily reflect the position of the Bruderhof.)

ISBN: 978-087486-283-6

Originally published in German as *Damit Gott kommt: Gedanken aus dem Reich Gottes* (Giessen: Brunnen Verlag, 1992).

A catalog record for this book is available from the British Library.
Library of Congress Cataloging-in-Publication Data

Names: Blumhardt, Christoph, 1842-1919, author. | Bittner, Wolfgang J., editor.
Title: Make way for the spirit : my father's battle and mine / Christoph Friedrich Blumhardt ; edited by Wolfgang J. Bittner.
Other titles: Damit Gott kommt English
Description: Walden NY : Plough Publishing House, 2019. | Series: Blumhardt source series
Identifiers: LCCN 2019019060 | ISBN 9780874862836 (pbk.)
Subjects: LCSH: Blumhardt, Johann Christoph, 1805-1880. | Blumhardt, Christoph, 1842-1919. | Lutheran Church--Doctrines--History--19th century. | Lutheran Church--Doctrines--History--20th century.
Classification: LCC BX8065.3 .B5813 2019 | DDC 284.1092/2 [B]--dc23
LC record available at https://lccn.loc.gov/2019019060

Contents

Series Foreword

THE BLUMHARDT SOURCE SERIES seeks to make available for the first time in English the extensive oeuvre of Johann Christoph Blumhardt (1805–1880) and his son Christoph Friedrich Blumhardt (1842–1919), two influential religious figures of the latter half of the nineteenth century who are not well known outside their native Germany. Their influence can be detected in a number of important developments in nineteenth- and twentieth-century Protestantism: the recovery of the eschatological dimension of Christianity and the kingdom of God; the recovery of an emphasis on holistic notions of spirituality and salvation; the rise of faith healing and later, Pentecostalism; the convergence of socialism and the Christian faith; and the development of personalist models of pastoral counseling.

Their collected works make available their vast body of work to scholars, pastors, and laypeople alike with the aim of giving the Blumhardts a full hearing. Given the extent of their influence during the theological and religious ferment of the late nineteenth and early twentieth centuries, we believe that these sources will be of great interest to scholars of that period across various disciplines. It is also true, however, that there is much spiritual and theological value in the witness of the Blumhardts. We hope that by making their witness more widely known in the English-speaking world the church at large will benefit.

The project outline is flexible, allowing for volumes that aim either in a scholarly direction or towards the thoughtful lay reader. The emphasis will be to reproduce, with only slight modifications, the various German editions of the Blumhardts' works that have appeared since the late nineteenth century. A modest scholarly apparatus will provide contextual and theologically helpful comments and commentary through introductions, footnotes, and appendices.

During their long ministries, the elder and younger Blumhardt found themselves called to serve as pastors, counselors, biblical interpreters, theologians, and even politicians. No matter the vocational context, however, both understood themselves as witnesses to the kingdom of God that was both already present in the world, and also breaking into the current structures of the world. Together they represent one of the most powerful instances of the convergence of spirituality and social witness in the history of the Christian church. As series editors, it is our conviction that their witness continues to be relevant for the church and society today. We hope that the current series will give the Blumhardts a broader hearing in the English-speaking world.

Christan T. Collins Winn and Charles E. Moore

Preface to the English Edition

Christian T. Collins Winn

IT WAS INEVITABLE that Christoph Friedrich Blumhardt would live in the shadow of his well-known and beloved father, Johann Christoph Blumhardt. His father came to the attention of wider circles after a small revival occurred in his southwestern German congregation following a purported exorcism, and as a result became a widely respected pastor and spiritual counselor throughout Germany, France, and Switzerland, and was even known in Great Britain and the United States.[1] The events surrounding the sickness and eventual recovery of Gottliebin Dittus, a parishioner in Blumhardt's congregation in Möttlingen, became the stuff of horror stories when details of the episode were eventually spelled out by the elder Blumhardt in his report to the church consistory.[2] The otherworldly drama had ended when Dittus's sister Katharina, who was starting to show similar symptoms, cried out in a voice "not her own": "Jesus is victor!"[3] This phrase became the central watchword of Johann Christoph Blumhardt's subsequent ministry.

Not long after, a renewal movement began within Blumhardt's congregation. Rather quickly, people far and wide began to journey to see Pastor Blumhardt, confess their sins, receive absolution – a rite of some controversy

---

1 See Dieter Ising, *Johann Christoph Blumhardt: Life and Work, A New Biography* (Eugene, OR: Cascade Books, 2009); and Christian T. Collins Winn, "The Blumhardts in America: On the Reception and Significance of the Blumhardts for American Theology," *Pneuma* 38 (2016): 1–25.

2 See Johann Christoph Blumhardt, *Der Kampf in Möttlingen*, in *Gesammelte Werke von Johann Christoph Blumhardt*, series I, vols. 1 and 2, edited by G. Schärfer, P. Ernst, and D. Ising (Göttingen: Vandenhoeck & Ruprecht, 1979).

3 See Friedrich Zündel, *Johann Christoph Blumhardt: A Biography* (Walden, NY: Plough Publishing House, 2019), 117–157; and Ising, *Johann Christoph Blumhardt*, 162–187.

in Lutheran circles – and listen to his compassionate, visionary, and stirring sermons. This did not please church officials, since parishioners were abandoning their local parishes to travel many miles to see Blumhardt. So, after some negotiation, Blumhardt ceased accepting visitors for pastoral counseling and refrained from offering absolution or prayers for healing.

Eventually even this restraint was not enough, so Blumhardt decided to step down from parish ministry. With the help of a generous benefactor, Blumhardt was able to purchase a recently restored spa, Bad Boll, and convert it into a spiritual retreat center. Meanwhile, Gottliebin Dittus and her siblings had joined the Blumhardt household, becoming indispensable in Blumhardt's ministry.

Christoph Friedrich Blumhardt was born in 1842 and grew up in the midst of these remarkable events. He was even a recipient of a good bit of "mothering" from Gottliebin Dittus, who by all accounts was a stern, powerful, and lively individual. After Christoph took over from his father in 1880, it was not long before those in the original group that had experienced the events in Möttlingen had all died: Dittus in 1872, Johann Christoph Blumhardt in 1880, and Christoph's mother, Doris Blumhardt, in 1886. When Hansjörg Dittus, Gottliebin's older brother, died in 1888, the last of the "Möttlingen generation" was gone.

It is not surprising that Christoph Blumhardt would turn in a new direction as the "Möttlingen generation" faded, or that a new focus would emerge. Already by 1886, following his mother's death, Blumhardt struggled for a new direction.[4] By the time Hansjörg passed away in 1888, Blumhardt described undergoing a kind of "inner pause."[5]

The first inklings of a possible change appeared after Blumhardt suffered a serious illness in 1889. Christoph noted that God was calling him away from the ministry of healing with which Bad Boll had become almost synonymous, saying, "Time and calling change, and we do not please God by always clinging to the old and customary ways, but by paying heed to the signs that show us new ways."[6] Precisely where Blumhardt was heading was not yet clear, but some of the reasons for the change were human selfishness and preoccupation with health for its own sake, rather than an openness to see instances of healing as signs of what God intended for the

4 See Christian T. Collins Winn, *"Jesus is Victor!" The Significance of the Blumhardts for the Theology of Karl Barth* (Eugene, OR: Pickwick Publications, 2009), 113–116.

5 See Simeon Zahl, *Pneumatology and Theology of the Cross in the Preaching of Christoph Friedrich Blumhardt* (London: T&T Clark, 2010), 39–40.

6 Christoph Blumhardt, *Eine Auswahl aus seinen Predigten, Andachten und Schriften*, vol. 2, edited by R. Lejeune (Zurich: Rotapfel, 1925), 127.

whole of creation. As he stated it: "I must frankly admit that for a long time already I have not felt happy about the increasing number of personal talks and letters in which health – and often only health – was eagerly sought from me through prayer. A great deal of misuse has resulted from this, as well as from all kinds of teachings and institutions which permit healing through prayer to seem a meritorious work in its right; healings which many were excessively elated over, or even proud of."[7] This change was but a first step towards reimagining the relationship between God's spirit, the kingdom of God, and the living Christ on one side, and the institutional church on the other.

The next step appeared in 1894, when Blumhardt decided to no longer function as a pastor at Bad Boll, laying aside his title. In his New Year's meditation of January 1, 1894, Blumhardt stated, "Now, for my part, as I am the one who must do that which can best serve peace, I am determined to allow a change to come into my house and into the work within it in the course of this year. I feel driven to develop precisely these thoughts which I have shared here. If I can operate more freely simply as *housefather* I do not feel any obligation to be the *pastor* in my house. I have decided to detach from my person all the importance of an ecclesiastical title."[8] Consequently, in the following years Blumhardt, as Timothy Scherer notes, "preaches less often, the communion is replaced by a communal meal, and baptisms and confirmations cease. Blumhardt's congregation in Bad Boll gradually gives up all the special rights and entitlements of a church. Parishioners now have to attend the other Lutheran congregation in Bad Ball in order to receive the sacraments."[9] The problem – stated even more clearly in the present text – was that ecclesiastical practices (whether ritual, hierarchical, or dogmatic) had arrested the power and flow of the Holy Spirit, which always longs to do something new in creation.

But what of Bad Boll and its traditions and history? Was Blumhardt's turn away from the church only another iteration of the sectarian spirit that often expresses itself in Protestantism? Did Blumhardt prefer the traditions of his father and Bad Boll over the traditions of the church? In light of the earlier move away from the healing ministry of Bad Boll, the answer to this last question would seem to be no – and for anyone who does not see the answer, this book will make it quite explicit.

---

7 Christoph Blumhardt, *Eine Auswahl*, vol. 2, 128.

8 Christoph Blumhardt, *Eine Auswahl*, vol. 2, 444.

9 Timothy Scherer, "Christoph Friedrich Blumhardt: Delivering Love in the Political Activity of an *Allerweltschrist*," (Ph.D. Dissertation, Fuller Theological Seminary, Pasadena, CA), 108.

For observers and participants in the broader ministry and network of Bad Boll, something seemed amiss. Blumhardt himself felt obliged enough to explain the potential direction that his ministry appeared to be taking, and how this new direction related to the established structures of Protestant Christianity, as well as to the expectations and ministry of his beloved father. So, over the course of 1895, Blumhardt penned this book, which he called *Gedanken aus dem Reich Gottes* (Thoughts on the Kingdom of God), and published sections in issues of his *Vertrauliche Blätter*, a circular newsletter for the Bad Boll network that included readers in Germany, France, and Switzerland. When the last section was published in December of 1895, the publication of the *Vertrauliche Blätter* also came to an end, marking another transition in Blumhardt's life and ministry.

Blumhardt's Evolving Perspective

THIS BOOK DEFINITELY CLARIFIES Christoph Blumhardt's position vis-à-vis his father, Pietism, and the broader Protestant church. Blumhardt discerns that his shift is entirely in keeping with the basic spirit and expectations of his father, though with some nuanced differences. The primary ostensible difference can be boiled down to Christoph Blumhardt's feeling that his father was too bound by institutional or traditional Christianity, unable to loosen himself from its grip, especially in regard to doctrinal teaching and to the significance of the church as the realm of the Spirit. And, from Christoph Blumhardt's perspective, his father was far too deferential to the ecclesiastical authorities. For the younger Blumhardt, Möttlingen exposed the relativization of the institutional church, which had become complicit with the power of death and its various modern expressions. Critiques of nationalism, capitalism, exploitation, deprivation, poverty, war – all these bubble just below the surface of the text, waiting to come out in Blumhardt's subsequent preaching as he moved closer to joining the workers' movement and the socialist party in 1899.

The text offers a unique marker for understanding Blumhardt's own development, but it is also of great interest in its own right. Offered here is a significant contribution on the role that the experience of the Holy Spirit should play in theological thinking and especially in the action of discipleship, vis-à-vis established practices and doctrines. How does the new wind of the Spirit relate to old structures?

Another significant theme is a theology of history that attempts to avoid the schematics that developed over the course of Christian history, finding especially powerful expressions in varied forms of nineteenth-century chiliasm. God is alive, the kingdom of God is present, and the Spirit does indeed move in and through history in concrete ways. But any and every moment of irruption can only be discerned as a "station on the way" to the final goal, which only God can bring. Yet for that goal to appear, human cooperation is necessary – even if only expressed in a longing for the kingdom of God to come.

Furthermore, the Spirit does not blow powerfully among Christian circles because they have made peace with death and its various manifestations – even allowing the Christian gospel to be distorted into a message of heavenly bliss in the hereafter. For Blumhardt, God's final Sabbath intention, that flourishing and irrepressible life will completely overcome death, is not something to be put in an appendix under the heading "after life." No, it can be experienced in the here and now in penultimate ways. When the ultimate comes, it will mean the transformation of everything and everyone. In the meantime, people of faith are called to the labor of prayer, struggle, and discipleship.[10]

This is the expansive vision that Blumhardt begins to spell out in these pages and which would take on clearer contours as his ministry and work continued, particularly among the working class.

On the Present Volume

THE PRESENT TRANSLATION is based on the edition of Wolfgang J. Bittner, which is based on the complete 1895 edition. The chapter titles and section headings are not original to Blumhardt. Originally crafted by Bittner, they have been retained for the reader's convenience but have also been reworked to better reflect the actual content that follows. We have also retained Bittner's introduction and afterword because they provide additional background on the text at hand, including some historical details regarding Blumhardt and the text that will be especially helpful to nonspecialists.

Finally, a note regarding an issue of translation: Blumhardt's use of the word *Fortschritt* deserves some explanation. Attempts to explain both the elder and the younger Blumhardt in the light of larger cultural, philosophical, or theological categories have sometimes used this term, which can be translated as "progress," as an indication that both Blumhardts were

---

10 For further discussion and analysis of the varied themes in this work, see Klaus-Jürgen Meier, *Christoph Blumhardt: Christ, Sozialist, Theologe* (Bern: Peter Lang, 1979), 35–44; Collins Winn, *"Jesus is Victor!"*, 129–136; Zahl, *Pneumatology and Theology of the Cross*, 61–84; Scherer, "Christoph Friedrich Blumhardt," 95–110.

more or less espousing the doctrine of "progress" that was dominant in the nineteenth century. This is particularly the case in regard to Christoph Blumhardt, since *Fortschritt* was one of his favorite terms for describing the movement of the kingdom of God into the future.

Though we cannot deny that Blumhardt was a child of his time, to assume that his conception of the forward movement of the kingdom and the Spirit is simply an assimilation of the dominant expectations of progress that marked the nineteenth and twentieth centuries is misleading and problematic. This is because Blumhardt speaks not so much about the forward movement of history, but rather about the movement of the kingdom of God. The latter can actually stall out even while the former continues in its own fits and starts. From Blumhardt's perspective, the forward movement of the kingdom stalls principally because the human proclivity to resist God's aims in the world actually bars God from giving both penultimate and the ultimate outpourings of the Spirit to rectify the world.[11] These aspects of Blumhardt's conception of the movement of history and the movement of the kingdom of God in history are sufficient enough to distinguish his thought from Hegelian conceptions of progress as well as more popular iterations. To retain this distinction, we have primarily translated *Fortschritt* as "forward movement" throughout the text.

---

11 For further discussion, see Zahl, *Pneumatology and Theology of the Cross*, 69–76.

Editor's Introduction

Wolfgang J. Bittner

GOD MARCHES FORWARD in history. If we want to live with God, we have to accompany him on this march no matter where it leads. Whoever stands still is in danger of losing God. "No one who puts a hand to the plow and looks back is fit for service in the kingdom of God" (Luke 9:62).

Christoph Friedrich Blumhardt wrote this book, which he titled *Gedanken aus dem Reich Gottes* (Thoughts on the Kingdom of God), in great haste. He wanted to explain to his closest friends his current (1895) standpoint regarding the experiences of his father, Johann Christoph Blumhardt. Similar thoughts from Christoph Friedrich Blumhardt have appeared in other books, but this book has been practically unavailable and pretty well unknown.

There must be a reason for publishing a new edition. Is it merely the reproduction of a historical text? No! Christoph Friedrich Blumhardt was a witness, and God gave him remarkably clear insight into what has validity for God's kingdom. Our time is different in many respects from his, yet today we are faced with events similar to those he had to take a stand to in his time. People were calling for revival and making reference to the elder Blumhardt's experiences. But were they appealing to Blumhardt's example without the deep surrender that recognizes God's right to their very being? That is, were they skirting around the renewal of their own lives? In calling for renewal, were they really interested in God and his rulership or in themselves? Was God able to freely assert his rightful claim in them or did they want God to help them implement the rights that they claimed?

Christoph Friedrich Blumhardt was a man of great intellectual and spiritual breadth and also a man of great inner depth. God leads to wide expanses. The dimensions of biblical hope that were opened up to Blumhardt are breathtaking. Blumhardt had hope for the present, for our everyday earthly world. He thought that to postpone this hope to the next world was dangerous, a treacherous curtailing of hope. God's promises are valid for the world as a whole, and they are valid for our physical life. Blumhardt fought against a Christian hope that had lost interest in this world, against a faith that had lost interest in our physical bodies. This is the only sense in which we can understand his involvement in politics and his commitment to the social problems of his time. If our hope is to keep up with God, we must hope until we expect the abolition of death right here in our earthly concerns.

Blumhardt's thoughts about renewal were never about strategy. He fiercely resisted any progress that was supposed to be doable in human strength. God leads us down into the depths. Blumhardt realized this more and more – in fact, the "Christian" person whose self-will has not been broken is truly more of an obstacle to the advance of God's kingdom than any sinister power from hell. It will depend on the small circle of believers whether or not Christianity is restored, whether or not the world is renewed. Are the people who are calling for renewal today really concerned about God? Or are we trying to help ourselves and merely hiding under the blanket of Christianity? God is not interested in helping people get their rights. He wants first of all for people to acknowledge his right to rule in their lives. That, then, is also the best help for them. God's way leads the same people who are calling for renewal to relinquish their lives again and again. They cannot bypass this surrender.

Depth and breadth are not opposites! They are both descriptions of the same path. Jesus knew and taught his disciples that God gives life from death. "Very truly I tell you, unless a kernel of wheat falls to the ground and dies, it remains only a single seed. But if it dies, it produces many seeds" (John 12:24). God's way has as its objective a broad horizon. But to reach this objective God's way goes through the depths. Christendom cannot escape that, nor can Christian renewal movements, no matter how hopeful and dynamic they may be. Whoever does not first take heed of the depths to which God wants to lead him will squander the breadth he was hoping for.[1] God himself went his way through history according to this rule and showed his Messiah that this was the way. Jesus affirmed this way and held his disciples to it. Whoever is looking for renewal that really comes from God must live accordingly. God leads through the depths to the breadths!

---

1 Deut. 32:39; 1 Sam. 2:6; Matt. 10:39, 16:24–25; John 12:15.

Who Were the Blumhardts?

THE FATHER, Johann Christoph Blumhardt (July 16, 1805–February 25, 1880), after serving as a vicar in Dürrmenz (1829–1830) and as a teacher at the Basel Mission (1830–1837), first was the vicar in Iptingen (1837–1838) before finally being appointed pastor at Möttlingen, near Calw, in July 1838. Through giving pastoral counsel to a sick young woman, Gottliebin Dittus, from June 1842 to December 1843, he was led to experience the healing of the sick and given an insight into the reality and power of the world of demons. Even more importantly, he also experienced the reality of victory in the name of Jesus. "Jesus is victor over all powers of darkness." That was the cry of victory which permeated and shaped the movement that followed. And was it ever a movement! A movement of repentance began that no one had foreseen, let alone consciously initiated. First the whole village was pervaded by the fear of God, then the next village, and soon the movement had spread throughout the region. People felt God's consuming holiness, which led them to repent deeply and start a new life in tangible ways. Healing and godliness became one.

Blumhardt's activity as a pastoral counselor soon exceeded the limits of a village pastorate. He recognized God's leading in this. The purchase of the Bad Boll spa gave him the space and opportunity he needed to care for sick and searching souls. Blumhardt became the housefather of a large communal family. All visitors were welcomed as a matter of course. He retained the rights of a pastor for the congregation in his house – in fact, he always tried to uphold his connection to the Lutheran church.

The salient features that shaped Blumhardt's life and work have remained alive in the memory and consciousness of Christianity. Because Gottliebin Dittus was healed, believers realized that healing the sick is just as much a part of the church's task as preaching the word. This idea had long been buried. The firsthand experience of dark, demonic powers and the extensive view into the kingdom of darkness provided the background against which the bright light of this jubilant realization flared up: God has promised us victory in the name of Jesus, his Son, and indeed he gives it to us even now. The far-reaching revival movement gave Blumhardt a hope which spanned the world, a hope that burst all confines: God wants to renew the whole world! But this hope was linked with prayer and the ever-growing certainty that God has to pour out his Spirit on humankind again and to a degree as yet unknown. Revival is possible only when it takes place through God's own strength. All we can do is hope for it and, believing, pray for it.

Johann Christoph Blumhardt's ministry is a witness to God's power. We can see he received the strength from God that he hoped for. This fact, however, is at the same time an affront to a Christianity that is smug, sedate, self-satisfied, and withdrawn. Still, whatever Blumhardt spoke and wrote was mostly sympathetic and compensating. He did not make it his job to fit his experiences, recognitions, and hopes into the familiar form of normal Christian life. He simply hoped that the church would be changed through the new experiences of the Spirit that God wanted to give her, so that she herself could be the bringer of a movement of renewal. He had to see that this was not so. The church remained the same as she was.

And what about the people who gathered around Blumhardt at Bad Boll? Did they turn out to be the bringers of a new movement? Blumhardt may have hoped and prayed for this. His son Christoph, too, strove for it for a long time. But what he saw – and increasingly felt to be the worst destroyer – was the way in which an experience of the Spirit again and again got tied up with the selfishness of pious people. It was not resistance from without that crippled any progress; it was the very Christians who had had deep experiences of God. They wanted to use God's power for themselves. When it came to making themselves available, without reservation, to the living God for his service to the world, they fiercely resisted. Instead of carrying God's hope into the world, they preferred to withdraw into "closed circles, separate from other people, and you know that this is the soil on which the worst Christian flesh grows. This flesh (unless it dies first) is capable of destroying Christ's spirit."[2]

With good reason we see unity in the ministries of father and son Blumhardt. But it is unity within diversity. Characteristics that strike us as sympathetic and compensating when coming from the father turn out to have corners and sharp edges coming from the son. Issues addressed by the father could be overlooked or disregarded if you didn't want to accept them, but these same issues coming from the son are pointed and unavoidable. The father's life appears to be a cohesive whole with a consistent approach, whereas the son's life can easily be divided into different periods.

Christoph Friedrich Blumhardt (June 1, 1842–February 8, 1919) was born shortly before his father's "battle" for Gottliebin Dittus began. He grew up as a rather shy child in an environment marked by constant wrestling and hoping for God's help. God's intervention was taken for granted as a natural part of dealing with the varied needs of daily life. These needs flowed in,

---

2 Christoph Blumhardt, *Eine Auswahl*, vol. 2, 585.

first to the parsonage in Möttlingen and later to Bad Boll. Christoph studied theology at his father's request, not because of any inclination on his part. After serving as vicar in several places, he returned to Bad Boll in 1869 to help his father, becoming his assistant and, eventually, his successor.

We cannot emphasize enough the influence Gottliebin Dittus had on Christoph Blumhardt. He himself only hinted at it. He says he owed to her "the ability to be broken without becoming a broken individual. No fiber was spared. You had to yield to her iron will." Her death on January 26, 1872, was a turning point in his life. At her deathbed he experienced that "remarkable birth" which he referred to occasionally in later years:

> A greater battle was fought that night, which ended again with: Jesus is victor! And that's why we live as we do to this day. This much has remained unchanged: our living connection to the Lord Jesus, who does not rest on behalf of the earth and its people, but accompanies them forward step by step and lets his children on earth feel the impact of his victory.

When Johann Christoph Blumhardt died in 1880, Christoph Blumhardt became the housefather. "There was a great outcry from innumerable people, telling me by letter or verbally that now the religious pleasures they had enjoyed every year, provided by my father, were at an end. I was overcome by silent rage: Is that the fruit of the life of a godly man, that in the end everyone just laments because they think they have to go without certain religious pleasures? Isn't God's kingdom greater than the man who worked for it?" The son received strength and wisdom to continue his father's work in the strength of God. Soon people even said, "It feels like the old pastor never died." This was the spirit in which Christoph Blumhardt continued to work at first. This period lasted until the spring of 1888. Robert Lejeune, the first to publish an extensive selection of Blumhardt's writings, used the Möttlingen slogan "Jesus is victor" to characterize this period.

In the first period we can already see signs of what becomes powerfully evident in the second period: God's help and God's blessing are never given to us as an endorsement that we should continue doing things as we have in the past. God's power leads to repentance. We have to fight with determination against anything in ourselves that wants to be independent of God, even if it is good and pious. God is looking for people who are not interested in themselves but in God and his honor; he needs people who let themselves be set on fire by God's hope for the whole world.

Difficult experiences in the household, in his family circle, and in his own life led Blumhardt to the slogan which permeates this second period: "Die, and Jesus will live." It was a time for serious judgment of oneself. Blumhardt wanted to lead his family, coworkers, and friends into a time of deep-going purification. The book we are reprinting here is the most conclusive writing for this second period, which ended soon afterwards, about 1896.

The third period shows a different face. For Christoph Blumhardt, still intent on reaching out, the ring of judgment dies away. The certainty of "God's love for the whole world" takes shape more and more clearly, molding Blumhardt's ministry and his life.

Blumhardt looked passionately for truth and for movements working for change. He felt that any movement which bore truth must come from God. This led him to join the Social Democratic Party of Württemburg in 1899, and he became their representative in the Württemburg Provincial Diet from 1900 to 1906. He never glorified this movement, but he acknowledged that here were people who, though they didn't speak of God, were closer to the truth than representatives of the state church who referred to God and his word but had become blind to the injustices and inequalities in the world. We can hardly imagine today what that meant within the political landscape of that time and the existing form of church involvement. Blumhardt believed that movements of God convey God's love to the world and that is why he joined them. After Blumhardt was elected, church authorities asked him to lay down his pastor's title. This did not surprise him – it was certainly characteristic of the church. As far as he was concerned, laying down this title merely gave him greater freedom to follow God. So even though the motto "God's love is meant for the world" was not coined by Blumhardt, you can feel his heart in it.

Blumhardt refused to be reelected to the Provincial Diet. The year 1907 marked the beginning of his withdrawal into quietness, which continued until the end of his life. It was not only a withdrawal from active politics. Because of serious illnesses he gave up the full responsibility for Bad Boll. He spent his last years at his house, called Wieseneck (meadow corner), in Jebenhausen, near Göppingen. However, from there he kept in touch with Bad Boll and regularly preached the sermon at Bad Boll for the next ten years. This last period of his life was marked by an increasingly quiet hope, which in stillness grew stronger and more convinced until it encompassed the whole world – "God's kingdom is coming!"

The Illness and Healing of Gottliebin Dittus

CHRISTOPH FRIEDRICH BLUMHARDT REFERRED again and again to what happened in Möttlingen with Gottliebin Dittus. "Möttlingen is our birthplace. Möttlingen influences the way we live even today. I don't know where we would be without Möttlingen. Möttlingen is the ground on which we stand and thrive. That is where the Savior opened the door that is still open."[3] In this book, he refers to these events frequently. But he could assume that his readership was familiar with what happened there. So to help the modern reader, I will give a brief sketch here of the most important occurrences.

Johann Christoph Blumhardt took up his work as a pastor at Möttlingen in July 1838 and was married in September of the same year. On the surface his congregation appeared to be devout and positive enough. But inwardly many were unmoved. Blumhardt's predecessor had told him that the congregation had been "preached to death." They regularly slept through his sermons. But how do you wake up a congregation? Blumhardt did not have to look for a way. It was unexpectedly laid at his feet in the person of Gottliebin Dittus, a gifted young woman, unmarried, who lived in the village with two of her siblings. In addition to various maladies, including a limp, an increasing number of strange phenomena started to occur, which the people said were spooky. The longer this continued, the more people in the village and beyond got to know about it. Counseling, prayer, and reading the Bible only seemed to make it worse.

June 26, 1842, turned out to be a decisive turning point. Blumhardt was called on this Sunday evening to come to Gottliebin, who lay unconscious after terrible symptoms. At that moment Blumhardt realized "something demonic was at work here." Then he was gripped by a kind of wrath:

> I sprang forward, grasped her cramped hands, forcibly placed her fingers together, as in prayer, and loudly called her name into the unconscious girl's ear, saying, "Put your hands together and pray: 'Lord Jesus, help me!' We have seen long enough what the devil does; now let us see what the Lord Jesus can do!" After a few moments she woke up, prayed those words after me, and all convulsions ceased, to the great astonishment of those present.[4]

This was the beginning of a struggle that lasted (with sometimes appalling manifestations) until the end of December 1843. Times of quiet alternated with severe and increasingly serious "attacks" that I will not describe here.

---

3 Christoph Blumhardt, *Eine Auswahl*, vol. 2, 14.

4 Zündel, *Johann Christoph Blumhardt*, 127.

The gruesome realities of witchcraft and magic were revealed to Blumhardt. It is hard to imagine how Blumhardt and his wife, Doris, survived this time. Their saving grace was that during this whole time they learned to trust in the power of the name of Jesus more and more. They sought for direction in prayer and by reading the Bible. They did not resort to any manipulation or medicines – they relied solely on the prayer of faith and later on fasting and reading Bible verses. They became increasingly convinced of the following: if Jesus helps us, we will be helped; if he does not help us, any other help will be our undoing.

In this way, Blumhardt went through the depths during this time, which led him into a breadth that he hardly noticed at first. Gottliebin was healed and freed from demonic possession once and for all around Christmas 1843, just a year and a half after the struggle began. The signal for the end, which came after frightful manifestations, was the harrowing howl that issued from the mouth of Gottliebin's sister Katharina, saying, "Jesus is victor! Jesus is victor!" That was the end of the struggle for this family. They were completely free, and this showed clearly in their emotional and physical recovery.

This ending proved to be a new beginning. People grew so troubled by their sins that they came to Blumhardt for confession without any prompting on his part. This was the beginning of a movement of repentance and revival that went far beyond the locality of his congregation.

Blumhardt had no intention whatsoever of publishing an account of his experiences. But because of the impact of these events, the news spread of its own accord. It spread so far that the church authorities demanded an account from the pastor. In August 1844, Blumhardt, with a heavy heart, gave the Stuttgart church authorities a thorough report, labeled "confidential." Copies of this report were soon circulating, without Blumhardt's knowledge. Although Blumhardt did not want further circulation, he agreed to have his account published in 1850. In addition to this publication, there are several smaller statements and the comprehensive *Verteidigungsschrift gegen Herrn Dr. de Valenti* (Written Defense against Dr. de Valenti), which appeared in 1850. All Blumhardt's accounts have been carefully collected in the scholarly book *Der Kampf in Möttlingen*, with extensive commentary. However, the most widely read account is the one included in the biography of Johann Christoph Blumhardt by Friedrich Zündel, which first appeared in 1880.[5] This is based on Blumhardt's

---

5 Zündel, *Johann Christoph Blumhardt.*

Krankheitsgeschichte (Account of Gottliebin Dittus's Illness) and describes these events in detail.

Christoph Friedrich Blumhardt believed deeply that the events described in these accounts show the working of God. He felt they represented the birth of the movement in which he himself stood as his father's successor. It was a battle through which God himself initiated a new time.

And yet the son criticized his father. Why? In the son's opinion, what happened should have been kept secret by the small circle of those involved. The results of such an experience are self-evident, but the God-given experience which creates these results should be kept secret. According to the son, publishing what happened at Möttlingen was harmful for God's cause on earth, not helpful. It only drew people's attention to the sinister events, so they fixed their gaze on the past and not on the victory given by the living God, who wants to lead his people forward. People noted the secrets of darkness and became interested in them. Thus, they failed to realize that God wanted to use this victory to lead to more victories in completely different forms.

About This Book

JOHANN CHRISTOPH BLUMHARDT'S PASTORAL CARE, begun in Möttlingen and continued in Bad Boll, led to a lively and far-flung correspondence. In order to stay in touch with the many people and to answer questions of general interest he circulated a newsletter, *Blätter aus Bad Boll*, from 1873 to 1877. On January 1, 1882, the son started sending his own *Briefblätter*, or newsletter, to a wide circle of friends. He included sermons, devotions, answers to questions, and items of news. But gradually the son got the impression that only some of the old Bad Boll friends had inner understanding for the path he was taking. So, in spring of 1888, he started publishing *Vertrauliche Blätter für Freunde von Bad Boll* (Confidential Newsletter for Friends of Bad Boll), a series that he planned to publish at irregular intervals in a smaller format. It was confidential so he could use it as a venue to discuss issues with a smaller circle of friends and companions. Blumhardt probably initially planned to distribute both newsletters in parallel, but already by the end of 1888 he discontinued the *Briefblätter*. Anyone who desired could subscribe to the confidential newsletter and thereby count himself part of the inner circle around Blumhardt. The form and content of this newsletter really were confidential. Blumhardt no longer wanted to spend so much of his time filling the needs of pious consumers.

This and several other changes in the outward running of Bad Boll resulted in a slew of inquiries, even accusations against Blumhardt, implying that he had strayed from the foundation on which his father had stood. People said Bad Boll was not what it used to be. So in April 1895 Blumhardt started to write a series of articles for the confidential newsletter. He wanted to respond more fully to these objections to his new position.

These articles were published without titles or headings. Blumhardt did not foresee that his thoughts would expand far beyond the initial purpose. He also at first had not thought of discontinuing the confidential newsletter. But now these pamphlets followed in rapid succession: April 1895, chapters 1, 2, and 3; May, chapter 4; June, chapters 5 and 6; July, chapters 7 and 8; August, chapters 9 to 11; September, chapters 12 and 13; October, chapter 14; November, chapter 15; and in December the closing chapter 16 with a title page and a table of contents that included chapter and subject headings.

Blumhardt did not formulate these thoughts as a unified whole, well organized and polished. As he wrote, his thoughts rose above the original reason for writing to address fundamental issues such as: What progress can we hope for in God's kingdom? What stands in the way of this progress? The manner in which this book came into being, "in which I have tried to present my point of view," explains why there are some rough places and some repetition. By the end of 1895, Blumhardt published these essays as a book in itself. Back in September, he had already notified his readers:

> This year I hope to write two or possibly three more booklets to follow this one, and that will complete this presentation of my current position. Then the publication of these little booklets will stop, because I think I will have said enough, that is, unless some reason comes up for publishing something. For the time being, however, as I have already said, I feel that I have said enough. I would like to express the wish that you read again what has been published already.

The last pamphlet really was the last issue of Blumhardt's confidential letters.

An Overview of the Book

BLUMHARDT STARTS WITH HIS REASONS for writing (Introduction). Why was he withdrawing to a smaller circle of friends – as evidenced by the confidential newsletters? That didn't look like progress. Many people who belonged to the inner circle did not understand him. Why the changes in the running of the household at Bad Boll? Why the refusal to continue so readily and so universally to pray for healing for the sick? Why the urgent and sharp call to embrace judgment, the call to surrender one's own life? These questions stemmed from the feeling many of his friends had that the son had slipped off the foundation his father had laid. The basic theme, which Blumhardt develops in this book in various ways, is this: the foundation for both father and son is the same; but as for what should be built on that foundation, God gave the son more clarity than the father had.

In the first illustration (chapter 1), Blumhardt characterizes his father as a man of forward movement, a man who walked forward with God and did not get stuck. Yet even here, he starts to criticize his father, by saying that his father tried to fit God's ways into the traditional forms of church life. When this proved impossible, God moved on ahead of the elder Blumhardt. First the father and then the son realized that God wants to achieve new goals. The new time that God had given them held new slogans and gave new instructions to anyone who wanted to accompany God (chapter 2).

In chapter 3, Blumhardt compares God's history, from beginning to end, to a series of milestones along a path, a succession of stations. The basic problem – common to all times – is that people mistake whichever station they are at with the final goal and get stuck there. This hinders God's progress through history. After God has given people magnificent experiences, they prefer to take a rest and not go any further. Instead of looking ahead to God, who has moved on, they look back. The result is preaching that turns only to the past and knows nothing of God's direct intervention in the present. This preaching slowly loses power. This chapter is probably the most important one for understanding Blumhardt's view of God and history.

In chapter 4, Blumhardt looks at his father's actions and ideas that, for him, stand above criticism: The struggle in Möttlingen against the powers of darkness has a rightful place within God's kingdom and undeniably has meaning for today. Even more: God's history always involves people. Any growth or progress that really comes from God will inevitably take a struggle. Whenever people make themselves available to God, God's kingdom involves them in some form of fight. The son considered his father to be such a fighter.

In the next chapters, however, Blumhardt takes a critical look at his father's experiences and his conduct. Publishing the account of Gottliebin

Dittus's illness harmed the whole movement. It drew people's attention to the story and to the "interesting" occurrences emerging from the demonic world. The struggle did lead to a victory for pastoral counseling, but then people's attention shifted and they did not see the necessity of now giving themselves up completely for God's cause (chapter 5). The elder Blumhardt's deference to God's love for humankind and for the existing traditions in his church led him to make compromises which almost shipwrecked him (chapter 6). He realized this himself and came to the conclusion that only a new intervention on God's part, an outpouring of the Holy Spirit – above and beyond anything heard of to date – would be able to put Christianity (and humankind) back on its feet. His forward-looking hope convinced him of this (chapter 7).

But the movement in Möttlingen carried a defect within it right from the beginning, in spite of its enduring significance: people used it for themselves. They looked for their own salvation. Their selfishness was not broken – it persisted (cloaked in a pious mantle) as the criterion by which they shaped their lives. This led the son to take steps appropriate for his situation. He felt that me-Christianity is in direct opposition to a Christianity in which believers make themselves available to God, in which believers are willing to sacrifice themselves for God's cause (chapter 8).

The next two chapters discuss healing the sick in a biblical and modern context. Chapter 9 looks at physical healing, and chapter 10 at the relationship between body and soul, and between the role of doctor and pastor. Blumhardt takes a sober look at healing from two points of view: the hope God offers us and the adverse realities of the times we still live in.

Blumhardt was anything but an admirer. In the next chapter (11) he criticizes his father's relationship to the church authorities. Here again he considers fundamentals. What do we do when we recognize God's will and the way he wants us to go and it is in opposition to what church leaders require? Blumhardt even takes the problem to a deeper level: What do we do when there is a conflict between our love to our neighbor and our love to God?

Up to this point Blumhardt has mostly been looking back at what his father experienced in order to explain his own position – where he agrees and where he differs. Now he turns to his father's hopes. Here, too, he does not just accept his father's ideas; he also rejects some. Yet as before, his sole reason for criticizing is to clarify the essence of what his father wanted so that it carries weight.

First (chapter 12) Blumhardt makes the following clear: progress in God's kingdom is not manmade, not a human achievement. It is not true that the kingdom of God automatically grows out of pious, Christian conduct. The kingdom is not something humans can bring about, but God's creation. It is not a question of a natural process, as though one period in history grows into a more elevated and more perfect one. Here we see an eschatological doctrine of history portrayed as a doctrine of creation.

Next Blumhardt shows in broad strokes how revolutionary changes in biblical times were the work of God. However, even if we expect change for the future to come not from human achievement but from the creative hand of God, we still have to imagine in concrete terms what we are hoping for. So Blumhardt outlines his father's three hopes for the future (chapter 13) – the future that will come from the hand of God and the future by which he oriented his life. The son feels, nevertheless, that the father supported his hopes with three false "staffs," and that these staffs curtailed his hopes and diffused their power. He hoped for a new outpouring of the Holy Spirit, and the institutional church was the false staff that intervened; he hoped for the formation of a new Zion, and mission was the false staff that intervened; and he hoped for the abolition of death on earth, and Christians' hope for personal salvation was the false staff that intervened. According to Christoph Blumhardt, what we have to do now is recognize the false staffs and resolutely lay them aside in order to give free reign to the three hopes and hence to God's power to recreate and make history. So, in conclusion, Blumhardt devotes a whole chapter to each of the three hopes (chapters 14 through 16).

Tips for Reading

THIS EDITION IS BASED on the complete version compiled into a book by Blumhardt at the end of 1895, though he never released it to the book trade. Readers may be assured that they have Blumhardt's unabridged text in front of them. Admittedly, the book can be challenging to read; some of Blumhardt's observations are more readily applicable to our time than others, and some passages repeat or belabor a point. However, the intent of this book is to present Blumhardt's thought unfiltered and unvarnished.

Blumhardt used the Bible heavily in his thoughts and arguments. Rarely, however, did he give the reference he had in mind. As editor, I have added many biblical references that are obviously indicated by Blumhardt's text, without attempting to be exhaustive. The chapter titles and section headings are also my addition.[6]

If anyone would like to get an overview of the important sections or acquaint themselves with Blumhardt's train of thought before reading the whole book, I would recommend chapters 3, 12, and 13. Chapters 14 to 16 and chapter 11 are also good starting points. In the afterword I briefly outline the theological content.

Blumhardt was not a polished speaker or writer. He consistently said what he thought without worrying about whether he might be misunderstood. The introduction and afterword should help you at least to discover the breadth of Blumhardt's thoughts. No matter how you look at it, his thoughts are challenging. Some passages that seem exaggerated to us today may have been occasioned by the situation Blumhardt was in, which is history for us. But is what Blumhardt faced and endured really only for the past? I would ask the reader not to attempt to put Blumhardt in a box. You will not be able to. What seems strange and new to you could be a call that will lead you to truths that we, as individual Christians and as the church of Jesus Christ, need to recognize and start putting into practice.

---

6 These have been revised for this English edition.

PART I

The Creative Tension

Continuity and Change

Introduction

Christoph Friedrich Blumhardt

DEAR FRIENDS, I HAVE been told several times that much of what I have written in my confidential newsletters[1] is not easy to understand. People say they cannot grasp what I am trying to achieve or what my position is in these turbulent times, when faith is battling against unbelief, subjective Christianity against ecclesiastic orthodoxy, narrow-minded Pietism against fanatical religious trends. Many may be wondering which of these trends I fit into. Others may be hoping to find in these newsletters confirmation for their own views. Still others may already be antagonistic and so they will understand as little as the first group. I fully realize that not everyone will immediately agree with me on every point. I think I have given sufficient evidence of this by the fact that, of late, I have sent out my little leaflet to friends only occasionally, at irregular intervals, only when I felt I had to, and with a strong emphasis on the confidential nature of these publications.[2]

We had to make certain changes to previous customs in our life, changes prompted by new experiences, both inner and outer. I knew from the outset that even our close friends would not understand right away the new life that was thrusting itself upon us. What I could envisage was so clear and thrilling! I saw clearly how immature and inadequate our former ways were and I also saw clearly the new route we had to take. But I had to hold back until what I knew in my heart to be true showed itself outwardly in our life. To a certain degree this has now taken shape, even though it will need to continue to grow before we have done justice to the truth we have been shown.

---

1 Blumhardt's *Vertrauliche Blätter* were published at irregular intervals starting in spring 1888.
2 See Bittner's introduction, section 3, about the transition of the newsletter from *Briefblätter* (newsletters), which Christoph Blumhardt published from January 1882 until the end of 1888, to *Vertrauliche Blätter*, circulated from spring 1888 until December 1895.

Our little ship has reached somewhat calmer waters now. So, I am happy to be able to fulfill the wish expressed by many of my friends to provide a more coherent and comprehensive statement of what has been given to us and what is even now the driving force behind every detail in our life.

The Same Foundation

A PARTICULAR FOCUS of this book will be to show that I have not strayed (as some people think) from the foundation on which I have always stood. That foundation is too secure and too eternal – laid down not by human beings but by God – for a single pebble to be broken off. However, some houses built on this foundation turned out to be manmade products of their time. These had to be abandoned, even though in their day they may have been a refuge that felt like home. I am surprised that many of you are so frightened by the demolition of these manmade constructions that you fail to notice the solid foundation underneath, on which we are still standing. This proves to me just how important it was for God to shake us free of so much that is comfortable and of the flesh. Otherwise, in the end, even in our circles, temporary and practical arrangements would have started to look as though they had come from God. In which case we, too, would have become static, unable to meet the needs of changing times. Rigid forms kill the Spirit. You can see this in nature, in creation, where life is always found in moving organisms, not in locked drawers.

It is impossible for me to explain to our friends my present point of view without drawing on the experiences of my dear father, Johann Christoph Blumhardt. These are recorded in the biography written by my departed friend Zündel.[3] As I write the forthcoming issues of this confidential newsletter, I plan to include extracts from the biography (which will give more details) for those who do not have a copy.[4] The biography is almost completely out of print, but I couldn't bring myself to have it reprinted because, at least for the time being, I am not planning to make my new views on the biography available in bookstores.[5] Public opinion is governed by all sorts of different spiritual trends and intellectual interests, and I do

---

3   The first edition of the biography of Johann Christoph Blumhardt by Friedrich Zündel appeared in 1880. By 1887 there had been five editions. Unless otherwise noted, all citations come from the English language version: Zündel, *Johann Christoph Blumhardt*.

4   Evidently Christoph Blumhardt was planning to quote passages from Zündel's biography, but in fact there is not a single quote in the text that follows.

5   The book you have in your hands first appeared as ten issues of *Vertrauliche Blätter*, from April to December of 1895. Then, as of January 1896, it was available from Bad Boll as a booklet, published by Christoph Blumhardt himself. He never made it available to the book trade.

not want to provoke public opinion, which might turn against us. I cannot see any advantage for the kingdom of God in doing so. My hope is that the insights we have been given may unobtrusively stir others into action, here or there, wherever the news may go. Therefore I plead, especially with those readers who do not agree with me, not to start a public debate. However, I am ready to discuss any objections in this confidential newsletter.[6] I think this will serve the truth better than public conflict.

In this book I will be obliged to comment on certain key moments in my father's life from my current point of view and in light of my present experiences. Sometimes I will approve and sometimes I will have to amend. This is because recent experiences have put a new light on my father's original experiences, and from this vantage point we can see that some of what we all thought was significant has proven to be insignificant and must therefore be laid aside. In this new light I will also feel compelled to draw certain obvious conclusions from my father's experiences – conclusions that he shied away from, because it was not yet the time. Yet no matter how different our movement and direction may appear today, it will soon become evident that an unbroken chain of experiences has built a bridge from Möttlingen to the present, bringing to us new hopes. Our present situation and outlook is but one more link in this chain and cannot be separated from the earlier links.

Or, to use a different metaphor, imagine a river – even though the water continues to flow forward, it remains connected to its source. All along, one of my prime concerns has been not to lose the original character of this movement, because its origin has shown itself to be a source of living water. This living water came as one of God's revelations through Jesus Christ, who is Lord of all lords and whose absolute power again and again clears the way for the truth of God's kingdom. His absolute power is still at work today just as in the time of the apostles.

God Knows the Truth

ANOTHER IMPORTANT REASON for me to focus on our origins is because many of the key events in my father's life have been misunderstood and misused by a lot of people at the expense of the truth. I thank God that

---

6 Christoph Blumhardt was probably planning to discuss these issues with Bad Boll's friends using the semi-publice platform of these *Vertrauliche Blätter*. That never happened. The subject matter that he was presenting took on such importance for him that he continued to write very rapidly and obviously with a strong inner sense of urgency. After writing the leaflets that make up this book, Blumhardt did not write anything for the public for quite a few years.

he has preserved my ability to think independently. I thank God that he intervened in my life to help me renounce today things that we loved dearly, things that over the decades had come to seem right and good, but that turned out to be merely human and did not belong to God's kingdom.

One thing you should know: I am not interested in what happens to me or mine. In that case we would be opening ourselves up to human honor. All we want is to work for God's kingdom and nothing but his kingdom and his righteousness (Matt. 6:33). In doing this more and more fully, we are ready in the end to lose our own lives and count all things as garbage in order to gain Christ (Phil. 3:7–8) – the same Christ who conquers and is alive. He lives so that the life of all creatures will be swallowed up in his life. Their life will appear brand new on his Day, truly an act of creation by God the Father through the Holy Spirit.

1

The Foundation Remains

ANYONE WHO KNEW MY FATHER, Johann Christoph Blumhardt, superficially (without a deeper insight into the longings of his heart) could happily consider him conservative – even though his experiences had given him many new and enlightening insights into Holy Scripture. It was not difficult to discuss matters with him, even if your basic outlook was very different from his. God had placed in his heart a warm love for the whole world and for all people, and it radiated from him. This love allowed him to look beyond the specific principles and organizations of the different Christian churches, even when these were obstacles and when they forced him, on a personal level, into an increasingly lonely position. Undaunted, he continued to bring everything and everyone into the light of his hope for a new outpouring of the Holy Spirit, and he expected the Holy Spirit to accomplish all the changes he was yearning for. So he was able to rejoice and had great hopes for every person of faith. In fact, through this hope of his, he was able to reassure believers of many different backgrounds – they all felt strengthened by what he said.

A Man of Progress

BUT NO MATTER HOW CONSERVATIVE he may have seemed to many, in actual fact he was not like that at all. He had witnessed something else; he had seen into the future world; he had seen promises being fulfilled, which made him passionate for Jesus, the victor, the one who will turn the whole world upside down according to the will of God. At heart he was a man of progress. He may have worked thankfully and conscientiously within his given circumstances, but in his heart of hearts he looked forward with longing, day and night, for something new, something eternal, something prophetic, promised, and certain. In quiet times when we would sit together, never once did I see him satisfied with things as they were. He thought our contemporary Christian lifestyle was bleak and boring compared with the bright picture of God's kingdom that had emerged full of promise in his heart and soul. He felt this picture confirmed the hopes of the nations since earliest times.

On one hand, he was most faithful to the church as it was – its sacred writings and symbols, its views, and its worship. In all of this he considered himself to be a member of the church in Württemberg. Yet, on the other hand, you cannot really call him a servant of the church. He served the kingdom of God, the kingdom that he could not find realized in any church. He knew, however, that it does exist in spirit and in truth. He was conservative by conviction because he believed that God would do the revealing. Therefore, he did not expect any progress to come from men and women – only from God. This gave him the ability, for God's sake, not only to put up with a given situation, but even more, to take full advantage of it for the goals of God's kingdom.

New Wine and Old Wineskins

IT NEVER OCCURRED to my father to develop new doctrines, new organizations, or new forms in order to bring about new life and new fellowship. He was deeply impressed by what God had given in the Reformation through Luther, and so he did not presume to openly criticize the [Lutheran] church. He held to this church even though he felt that it was inadequate in many ways. Wherever he could, he tried to bring in some fresh life through the cracks in the old structure – for example, regarding intercession, confession, and deliverance from both physical and emotional bondages caused by demon possession. He held to this church even though it opposed him, put him down, and sought to quench his spirit. Because he had faith, he resigned himself [to things as they were] and waited for a new time that would come from God, for a new outpouring of the Holy Spirit. This expectation kept him on tiptoe, inwardly fresh and alive, ready for any step forward, ready to leave everything behind should God speak anew or should Jesus Christ give his heavenly Father's work a more perfect form.

Certainly, my father himself was not fully aware of how different the present state of affairs was from the future for which he yearned. His vision was still shrouded in many ways. God permitted him to first try and see if the present forms could be reshaped – if the existing vessels (the church's ordinances) would be able to hold that which he felt was needed for the future of God's kingdom. He just could not yet grasp that the church might, under certain circumstances, actually reject a living testimony coming from God and choose instead the existing ordinances. Therefore, he remained hopeful until his death that the church ordinances used by the people surrounding him would be able to incorporate his experiences. This is why, again and again and with extraordinary love, he tried to reconcile his own inner advances with the doctrines and forms of worship surrounding him and even to justify the old ways.

New Attempts and Failures

IN HIS ATTEMPTS TO ACCOMMODATE, my father wrote several testimonies, such as the "Fifteen Advent Sermons,"[1] which lost a lot of their verve simply because he was trying to harmonize the more liberated outlook and more Spirit-filled life that God had given him with traditional, dogmatic forms of doctrine, church traditions, and customs. You could say that my father was still caught in the shackles of [traditional] theological work – fetters that have entangled Christians voices since ancient times. People often look for salvation by trying to find answers to questions that basically are none of our business. I remember, for example, the debate on eternal salvation and eternal damnation, to which my father devoted an excessive amount of time in deference to some church teaching or other. I must admit that he defended his beloved traditional church viewpoints with an eloquence that would have been more appropriate for the profound, eternal thoughts that lay in his soul.

But I do not want to belittle his efforts to merge the new with the old, the essential with the nonessential. He was trying to bring about a general consensus as a basis on which faith and hope could be further developed. The benefit of using conventional methods of theological thinking and research was that he won the support of a large, open-hearted circle in which his hopes caught fire. This circle inevitably became liberal (in spite of my father's loyalty to conventional ways) because progress was simply in him. In fact, this power to advance was stronger than he was and led him beyond what he could possibly have foreseen.

After all, the people in more narrow-minded circles, whom he solicited with such love, did not in the end regard him as one of their own, while

---

1 *Fünfzehn Predigten über die drei ersten Advents-Evangelien, zur Beförderung christlicher Erkenntnis* (Fifteen Sermons about the First Three Advent Gospels: to Promote Christian Knowledge), Stuttgart, 1864.

those in broad-minded circles, who allied themselves to him and his hopes for forward movement, found themselves isolated more or less everywhere because of those very hopes. Therefore, I say boldly that God did not let him get bogged down in conventional ways, no matter how much time and effort he sacrificed for it. In the end what he most deeply longed for, all his experiences and his hopes, were completely different from what other people wanted them to be. So my father did not end his life within the narrow framework of religious thought, but instead bearing in mind all peoples, for whom he saw God's kingdom coming in an undreamed-of and wonderful way. His last words were, "The Lord will open his hand in mercy toward all people!" These words do not fit into the narrow framework of any political party or specific people, nor into any existing church or state. They fit only into the wide horizons given to us by the Bible in the Old and New Testaments.

The Same Forward Movement

THIS SEQUENCE OF EVENTS was a milestone for me. I realized that my father's attempt to bring progress in the old ruts had failed. For years I, too, tried to find my way within the inner and outer circumstances handed down to me by my father. But when he died I knew that my task was to work for *the same forward movement* that motivated him.[2] And to this day those of us who know we were shaped by my father's struggle realize that we are being swept along by this progress. We have never tried in our human strength to uncover this or that little treasure; we merely longed and wrestled in prayer to God, hoping that he would lead us to new clarity. This much we knew for certain: If we stand still we will get separated from what God is saying today, from the living witness that is hammering on the doors of our world today.

This is exactly what happened. Today, whether we like it or not, we are prompted [by God] again and again and have to make new changes. Speculation will not help us to understand the kingdom of God; rather God uses definite experiences to give us new insights. Then, unless we are cold and dead, we have to change our views according to what we have just experienced. For this is how God guides his children on earth: he gives us

---

2 Christoph Blumhardt repeatedly emphasized that his father's death was an outstanding turning point. The anniversary of his father's death became a memorial day at Bad Boll. See for instance the devotions of the son for January 26, in Christoph Blumhardt, *Ansprachen, Predigten, Reden, Briefe, 1865–1917, vol. 1, 1865–1889*, ed. by Johannes Harder (Neukirchen-Vluyn: Neukirchener Verlag, 1978), 65–66.

tangible experiences of judgment and of grace – experiences which it would be a crime to pass over indifferently just to stay true to our old ways of thinking. If we compare today with yesterday and with bygone times, we can see that the same Spirit still compels us today – the Spirit who gave the inescapable summons that Jesus alone must be Lord. However, for the sake of this same Spirit we will from time to time have to suffer through entirely new experiences, which in turn will force us to take up new points of view. For how is Jesus to conquer, if everything has to stay the same as it was before? How is he to rule, if we are not willing to give up anything? How is he to be exalted, if we value our human lives more than we value him?

No Easy Path Ahead

A CHARACTERISTIC FEATURE of my father's life was that he repeatedly found himself thrust into something new, and each new chapter was more powerful than the previous one. As an assistant pastor he was blessed, and people were drawn to him. Even the most stiff-necked sectarians were won over to more reasonable, loving relationships within the parish.[3] This event gave his life a new momentum, and he might well have thought that with this new enthusiasm he had done enough. Then he moved to Möttlingen to be the pastor. Of what use to him here was his former position? His enthusiasm died down because the congregation was lifeless. As far as preaching goes, everything had already been tried by preachers better than he.[4] He grew sad when he realized that all his efforts were useless, even when he tried hard to relate to people in their day-to-day lives. He could not awaken any real love for God and his cause.

Then God stepped in and opened his eyes to see why even the most enthusiastic sermons did not hit their mark. He got a taste of the very depths of hell, for this is where the shackles originated that ensnared the entire congregation. Now every part of his life had to undergo change. What good would it do him to long for the happy days of being an assistant pastor? Now he had to take up a battle and forgo all comforts, until he heard the cry "Jesus is victor!" and his congregation was set free.[5]

Another man might have made it his life's work to continue battling in this way, but my father was faced with yet another change. Though quietly

---

3 See Zündel, 50–54.

4 Johann Christoph Blumhardt's friend, who preceded him as pastor in Iptingen, Dr. Christian Gottlob Barth, called the congregation a "congregation that had been preached to death." See Zündel, 99. What this meant for Blumhardt is described by Zündel, 108, 160.

5 About the end of the "battle" see Zündel, 151–152.

continuing the battle, he felt he had to do justice to the new circumstances that had developed. Suddenly he had to be a spiritual advisor in a totally new way, unlike anything he had ever dreamed of. He now had a congregation radiant in their first love. Was this not enough? No, this proved to be but a short-lived break. A number of experiences in his congregation made him realize full well that he would have to make another step forward. He challenged his congregation, "If we do not move forward, if we get stuck in the old ruts that all other converts have followed, the light will go out again!" But any progress that will require a restructuring of life can only come into being through a totally new working of God, through an outpouring of the Holy Spirit, by which former things are overturned and new things built up. Again new ground had been reached. The years at Möttlingen were definitely a highlight – a comfort and a light, a strengthening of his faith – but they were not the *goal*.

It was not long before my father felt he had to leave Möttlingen.[6] He must have been sad to abandon his congregation and set out into the unknown. It didn't happen without a crisis. My father was like a man going through bouts of fever, until he was weaned from his former role as the pastor of a congregation and felt comfortable in Bad Boll, where God placed him. It was essential for him to die to his Möttlingen. The fruit harvested there was not his doing and not for him to keep – it was God's doing and my father had to hand it over to God, the real vine dresser. He had to leave so as not to waste away in the narrow confines of a parish, caring for a few hundred people, or a single church, or even the larger circles of the Protestant church. God gave him a universal point of view that eventually rose above all confessions.

God's Time Changes

LATER, FOR THE SAKE of this universal point of view (that we had come to with my father) we had to put up with changes, both inner and outer. The spirit of life in Jesus Christ, which keeps us moving forward toward the final goal, forced us increasingly to take responsibility for much that still held us captive. God gave us evidence that he was at work – whenever we started to get too comfortable, he used all kinds of experiences to wake us up. The death of my father, as well as that of all the older members of our family and community (those who had experienced the early days), was reason enough to make us consider changes. If we wanted to be gripped by the truth and to seek for the truth, then we had to listen to what God

---

6 Not because of an external force but because of an internal "must." See Zündel, 388–392.

was demanding of *us*. We had to look at *our own* attitudes and get clear about what was from above and what was from below. At least we had to get to the point where we could say without hesitation, "We will not cling to anything we are used to. Instead we will be ready to work for anything that is true and just." For we have set our hearts on things above (Col. 3:1), and whatever is not from above, we will renounce even if it is dear to us. For only things from above belong to Jesus and are eternal. Whatever comes from below is not eternal and is at least able to cause great harm. On this basis we are willing to endure any changes – but we must watch out that we are not the ones to initiate change; that we continue to allow what we *experience* to lead us.[7]

So now we have come to *our* day, which we face with the same earnestness and the same zeal, the same confidence and inner certainty with which my father faced *his* day, fifty years ago at Möttlingen. In his day, the powers of darkness opposed him. He saw people chained in darkness and fought zealously for Christ's victory over evil powers. In our day, we have not forgotten this. We are well aware of the power of hidden forces. We know of the lingering inner bondages that still obstruct God's kingdom. But experiences in our day permit us to pay less attention to this. God has opened our eyes so we can see that it is our human selfishness which is resisting God – the selfishness called the flesh. If we can do away with this resistance, it will have even more important consequences than a victory over demons.

A New Watchword

THEREFORE, IN OUR DAY, we have to die, so that Jesus can live. This means that we want to be dead to whatever is human and to whatever focuses on people. Our human nature is not to be nurtured through God, through Christ, and through the Spirit – on the contrary, our human nature, our flesh, is to be revealed and judged through God, through Christ, and through the Spirit. For it is only in this way that we can come to the final forward movement: to a new creation, to a resurrection in terms of godly things, in the spirit of God's truth and righteousness. The first watchword was "Jesus is victor!" in the battle against darkness and superstition,

---

7 By "experience" the son Blumhardt is referring to daily events. He recognized God's speaking and leading in daily events. He attempted to understand them and to fit in with them. For a discussion of the son Blumhardt's conception of experience, see Simeon Zahl, *Pneumatology and Theology of the Cross in the Preaching of Christoph Friedrich Blumhardt: The Holy Spirit between Wittenberg and Azusa Street* (London: T&T Clark, 2010).

and later on the watchword was "God is merciful to all creatures, because Jesus is victor!" Today the watchword is "Die! For only then can Jesus live!"

He can only live and reign, be victorious and rise again, if you renounce what is yours and die to yourselves, so that you, being dead to yourselves, can come to God with your whole heart and your whole soul to bring forth that fruit which is pleasing to God. For only when people submit themselves in a totally new and more perfect way will that victory come which makes God's mercy possible for all creation. For, as I said already, Jesus does not want only victory – he wants life. He wants to live in you, in people who have flesh and blood, for the benefit of God's justice and truth on earth.

2

New Assignments

IF IN OUR DAY THIS WATCHWORD, "Die, and Jesus will live,"[1] has come to the fore, then certainly we will have to act differently than we did before. With the watchword "Jesus is victor!" we could launch into the fight, and our life was filled with a joyful, victorious faith and hope. It was a time when all eyes and ears were fixed on the enemy. It didn't matter if, in the meantime, we continued to use the existing forms and institutions in our personal lives. We were at war and so we had no time to think about our-selves. And since this war was fought mainly against invisible enemies, we had to be satisfied with Christianity as we found it. God called my father just as he was, and told him: "I am the victor, so do not be afraid of the devil, death, or hell!" So even when certain doctrines and ordinances of the church seemed at times to get in the way during such a battle, it did not mean we had to break with them. We could take them in stride, since the issue at hand was the external enemy.

Our situation today is different under the watchword "Die, and Jesus will live!" After all, that particular battle had to end at some point, and it has ended. Because, what are we really fighting for? Obviously not to continue fighting forever! If Jesus is victor, the time must come when the fighting stops – be it temporarily or permanently, a victorious armistice or a lasting peace.

Standing in God's Way

THIS IS WHAT our present situation looks like. At the moment we are no longer fighting against external enemies. Jesus, the victor, has led us home

---

1 cf. Matt. 10:39, 16:24–25; John 3:30, 12:24–25; Gal. 2:20.

and said, "Now put your own house in order, too. Since you fought so bravely against the enemy, I now want to see if you can also fight bravely against yourselves." As it stands today, we have to admit to our shame that we, who want to be disciples of Jesus, cause God almost more trouble than the enemy does. We are discovering sins in our lives, which have to be rooted out. A sharp wind is blowing against all kinds of familiar misconceptions and institutions that we used to accept as harmless. Now we have to admit that they did not sprout on the soil of truth. Much of what was precious and valuable to us in earlier days no longer meshes with the truth today. To all this we must die with Christ, and in many respects we must take the same position as the apostle Paul, who said, "I consider everything a loss . . . that I may gain Christ" (Phil. 3:8).

I am sorry that this dying with Christ offends and angers so many people in our neighborhood. But what should I do? I cannot help it if in many ways how we used to live doesn't correspond to the truth of our day. It is important to move forward in obedience to God, who is a God of truth and righteousness and who certainly does not want his kingdom to languish forever in untruth and unrighteousness. So we had to accept changes that make people accuse us of no longer acting the way my father did. But if we believe that God's kingdom is coming and is being fulfilled, then we cannot put our faith in our institutions and traditions. On the contrary, these have to be either changed or totally done away with from time to time according to the advance of God's kingdom.

The Insufficiency of Doctrine

LARGE CIRCLES OF PEOPLE make the mistake of thinking that to further the coming of God's kingdom, it is enough to have a doctrine which has been recognized and defined once and for all. This mistake is poisoning most people's understanding of God's kingdom. It is poisonous because then we start to give almost more importance to certain institutions and doctrines than to God himself. It is obvious that for the sake of such established institutions the truth is being set aside. Another error, equally obvious, is that our Christian mode of life is governed more by human laws than by divine laws. So we are expected to revere people and institutions and be more zealous for them than for God, even though we say at the same time: "Salvation is found in no one else, for there is no other name under heaven given to mankind by which we must be saved" than the name of Jesus (Acts 4:12).

We now see clearly that there is no single doctrine, dogmatically recognized and defined, which is decisive for God's kingdom, but only the living God. God's intervention at Möttlingen shook us and woke us up. Compared to before, we now are awake. We know that again and again it is important for us to stand alert at the door, so we can open it when the Lord comes (Rev. 3:20; Luke 12:36–37). For we have to be ready when he comes, not that God has to be ready when we come!

It has also become clear to us that this living intervention of God will not always repeat itself in the same way, nor take place mechanically by means of grace alone. Rather, God's intervention comes as a thief in the night (Matt. 24:42–44). We have to be ready for new situations and new responsibilities. God will lead and guide his people until the end of the world according to the times and the circumstances in which people live. It would make no sense at all for the Savior to say, "Surely I am with you always, to the very end of the age" (Matt. 28:20), if it were not necessary for him to intervene and govern. Since God is not simply a dead corpse, we too should be alive and flexible and not get strangled by temporal institutions. It pays to be open for surprises. It pays to make forward movement, to dispose of what is out of date, and to accept the contemporary. It pays to be armed against attack from within or without, so we can hear the orders of the commander in chief at the right time and in the right way. Of course there are also resting points, which we must reach one at a time amidst battle and temptation. But no one is granted a long-term break until the people of God reach their final goal – and then all peoples can be drawn into this circle of truth and righteousness.

Hastening God's Kingdom

IN THIS SENSE OF WAITING for and hastening toward the kingdom of God, my father's life continued nonstop. He was well aware that what he had accomplished was not the goal, neither for him nor for others, but only a path toward the goal. This basic attitude was engraved upon us, and so we also want to move forward nonstop. While acknowledging the eternal in what has been accomplished (while carrying and safeguarding it in our hearts), we still would like to expose our outer and inner life to God's judging eye. Then, freed of dross, we may be led forward through Jesus the victor on paths that lead toward the final goal. Jesus Christ describes this final goal as resurrection and life, as God's Sabbath, in which the life of creation purified in God blossoms into its true and right form.

Everyone who is seeking for the kingdom of God should bear this in mind, so that they do not cause others to have a grudge against or judge sharply those who have been switched from old grooves to new ways. Again and again we have to set our "hearts on things above, where Christ is, seated at the right hand of God" (Col. 3:1). This "above" has to count for us down here on earth, and for this to happen we have to remain flexible on earth. Otherwise we, with our own efforts, choke to death that which is from above.

3

Many Stations

IN EVERY AGE one of the greatest mistakes that people make (people who are called to be servants of God) is that when they arrive at a station they think it is the goal. Reveling in what they have accomplished, they lose sight of what could still be achieved. They are like foolish soldiers, who after their first victory just want to have peace and go back home, instead of wanting to gain the final goal through a last, decisive victory. In the same way, God's people became sluggish and settled down after their first insights into God's revelations; they did not care anymore about God's will for the whole, for the ultimate. Even though a few leaders pressed forward with loud cries, the vast majority of those who had arrived at a station were delighted to take a rest and refused to be involved in any further battle. Take for example those Jews, satisfied with their own orthodoxy, who only clung to the past revelation, in contrast to Simeon, who was burning for new revelation (Luke 2:25–35).

Stations on the Way

THIS IS WHY in the history of God's kingdom we usually see only sporadic advances toward the goal. It is much like an inert mass that even with force can only slowly be brought into motion. Ever since earliest times, God has insisted that forward advances be made according to his will. But we see that the very people who should understand and carry out the advance of his spirit of truth are in the dark. In spite of the fact that God was initiating advances for their time and circumstances, those whom he had called not only came to a standstill, but even retreated. This has been the painful postscript to every chapter in the history of God's kingdom. If, through God's grace and revelation, some of God's people reached a station, then to be sure they were granted a time of rest and refreshment, but only in the expectation that they would then head for the goal all the more zealously. Instead, giving in to listlessness and self-interest, they usually made themselves at home at that station and forgot about the goal.

God saw how decade by decade his disciples increasingly fell away and were ruined to the disgrace and detriment of his kingdom. We have to realize this – indeed, in a totally new way today – because people have fatalistically attributed this downfall to the will of God. We have to realize that we are at fault when people waste away on the stations of God's grace. We have to look for the guilt within ourselves. I hope to help people recognize this as much as possible, in order to relieve God of false accusations. Thoughtless people, knowingly or unknowingly, accuse God when the progress toward his kingdom has not yet brought about what he originally promised.

God Never Gets Stuck

ACCORDING TO SCRIPTURE there have been many such stations during the course of history. None of them were brought about by people – God himself brought them into being through his revelations to human beings, from Noah and Abraham up to Jesus. Again and again a new light dawned, but again and again the people called to the light came to grief through their own fault. Other people had to take their places and were put to the test. Would they adopt the most recent revelation that would lead to the goal? Jesus was the last, the key station and the brightest light (Isa. 9:2, 49:6; John 8:12) before God's great goal. In a comparatively short time, through the direct guidance of the Holy Spirit, the last goal was to be reached.

Nobody today would want to claim that Jesus or the apostles were deceived or were trying to deceive people when they proclaimed in their day that the fulfillment was close at hand. Nobody would consider the almighty God to be so slow or so long-winded that it would take him two thousand years to carry out his plans – plans already very nearly realized. Why has this goal, which was so imminent in the days of Jesus and especially after his resurrection, not yet been achieved? Please don't quote Bible verses such as: "Truly you are a God who has been hiding himself" (Isa. 45:15), or "A thousand years in your sight are like a day" (Ps. 90:4; 2 Pet. 3:8). For such talk only supports the laziness we are so fond of, which is in the flesh and blood of all of us. They support sin, which so easily entangles us

(Heb. 12:1). Or do we want to accuse the true and living God of wanting to inflict on us two thousand years of misery, after Jesus had given his apostles a completely different picture? No, it must be the fault of *us human beings* – we got stuck, not God.

Learning from Mistakes

THE BIBLE RECORDS MANY EXAMPLES of enlightened people who came to a standstill and got stuck, when God meant for them to press on. When Israel in the desert looked back and lusted for the fleshpots of Egypt (Exod. 16:3) and then looked forward and feared the battle for Canaan, it was not God's fault that they were delayed in the desert and that many died there, instead of entering the Promised Land (Num. 13–14). Even Moses was guilty of a mistake, through which he became co-guilty of the sins of his people (Num. 20:1–13). At a later time in Canaan, because the blessings of God's kingdom failed to materialize, the curses of paganism moved in and the entire history of Israel became permeated with pagan atrocities. The only forward movement toward salvation was in the spiritual realm through the prophets – while the people perished! Was this because God wanted the Messiah to come only when the entire nation was in ruins? Or because he wanted the people to fall into sin and error in order to gain time? No, it was the fault of the people themselves – even of respected men of God at that time, who became unfaithful and deserted their God (Judges 2:10–22). Just think of the devastating story of Solomon, a lover of God's kingdom, who arrived at a great and wonderful station, and then rotted in his happiness – he along with his people. As a legacy he left to the God of truth a nest of lies in the form of idolatrous temples and golden houses (1 Kings 11:1–13).

I will skip over many other stories but give as a last example the story of John and Jesus himself. John the Baptist was a herald, a station on the way to the new covenant. Only some of his disciples, however, were ready to adopt Jesus' totally new and different behavior. Even their teacher was in danger of being confused for a moment, and Jesus had to send him the message: "Blessed is anyone who does not stumble on account of me" (Matt. 11:6). Many thought they should continue doing just what John had done. They held to John so tenaciously that in Acts (19:3–7), and also later, "disciples of John" are mentioned. A sect lingered on just because of the stubbornness of John's early adherents.[1] Moreover, the question also came up, "How is it that

---

1 Christoph Blumhardt is referring to the sect of the Mandeans, who were followers of John the Baptist.

John's disciples are fasting, but Jesus' disciples do not?" (Mark 2:18). In other words, wouldn't it be better to stay at the station John reached?

Such stories are important for us, so that we do not make the same mistakes that have already been made so often. Jesus' disciples can also get stuck at the first pause in his revelation and not be quick enough to hear and follow new instructions. Therefore, I agree with the question that many scholars have raised through studying Acts. Wasn't there a certain bias among the first apostles, too, which caused them to get stuck in the powerful spiritual movement of the early days in Jerusalem? Didn't this delay or even prevent the appearance of Jesus Christ, the resurrected one? Let me say a little more about this.

Apostolic Stations

THE FIRST APOSTLES RECEIVED the outpouring of the Holy Spirit and through it an unexpected harvest among the Jews (Acts 2:41, 2:47; 6:7). Of course they were overjoyed that in spite of their master's verdict, condemning Jerusalem (Matt. 23:37–39; cf. Luke 13:6–9), a remnant was called to God's Zion.[2] Even though Jesus first told them to go to the Jews as much as possible, he never said they should stop with the Jews or only get involved with them. He also commanded the apostles to minister to the Gentiles and to all nations (Matt. 28:19; Mark 16:15). The tongues of fire and speaking in many languages (Acts 2:3–11) were the most obvious indications that this commission was henceforth meant not only for the Jews, but for all languages. That means all nations of the earth were called to be one sacrificial fire in the sanctuary of God.

But love for their nation got the upper hand. The apostles could not separate themselves from the Jews, even when disaster struck, as when Peter was thrown into prison (Acts 4:1–22, 5:18–19, 12:3–7) or when James was beheaded (Acts 12:1–3). Even though the vision of the unclean animals clearly showed Peter God's will in regards to the Gentiles and the nations (Acts 10:9–16), the apostles still clung to the idea that the kingdom of God could be firmly established only through the Jews. So to their shame God was compelled to take Saul and make him into Paul (Acts 9:1–22). Anyone who knows the New Testament knows how many adversities and shameful things happened after that, which resulted in two different kinds of

---

2 When Blumhardt uses the word "Zion," he means a group of people who are entirely at God's disposal, who disregard their own persons, thereby becoming part of God's salvation of the world. "Zion" is used in this sense of the world's final salvation in Isaiah 2:1–5 and 4:2–6. Blumhardt expands thoroughly on this idea in chapter 15.

Christianity. No one can cover up the fact that the apostle Paul had to work against great odds and that those who stood most in his way were exactly those who, confronted with the challenge to move beyond the Jews, could not do so.[3]

Confusing Results with the Goal

I WOULD LIKE TO MENTION a more spiritual point. Through the outpouring of the Holy Spirit, the apostles were put in a position where they could preach the gospel with accompanying signs (Mark 16:25–30). This is the good news which the apostles proclaimed, stated briefly: "Believe in Jesus, the resurrected one. Then the kingdom of God will come, which will redeem and reshape the whole world through the appearance of Jesus Christ." Their proclamation was divided into two parts. On the basis of the grace and revelation already granted, a further revelation was expected. Now the grace already bestowed was truly great: People who previously were completely incompetent saw themselves – gripped by the Holy Spirit – suddenly empowered to preach the gospel with the authority of God. They could preach the good news that in Jesus the kingdom of God was coming. They must have been highly elated when they became aware that their preaching, accompanied by signs and wonders, had such a powerful impact. They had arrived at a blessed station: in every direction a great ministry of preaching and working wonders was unfolding.

The apostles never entirely forgot the second part of the good news, and they certainly continued to press forward and urged their converts to work out their future salvation with fear and trembling (Phil. 2:12). But even in the apostolic period, many disciples thought that the grace and revelation which empowered them to preach the gospel was the final goal – hence any further striving for more grace and further revelations seemed unnecessary. You can sense, through the admonitions of the apostles to the churches, that some believers were much inclined to rest on the soft pillows of the grace they had received and were happy to leave everything else for God to work out.

Evidently the ability to preach and perform miracles was not the last gift of the Holy Spirit. This empowerment was meant to serve the church of Jesus Christ for the time being, for its spiritual development without spot or blemish, so that in the church a Zion of all peoples could come into being, a gathering place for all nations before God. We see clearly that the

---

3 See Acts 15. Unfortunately, over the course of church history, Christianity's bond with Judaism was lost almost entirely. This clearly was not what Paul intended (Eph. 2:11–22).

apostles did not suppose that their preaching by itself could bring about the conversion of all nations. They were well aware that they had been endowed only with the gifts to establish fellowships here and there among the nations. These fellowships were meant to lead a quiet life, somewhat withdrawn from the world (1 Thess. 4:11–12), and continue developing, growing spiritually in the knowledge of Jesus Christ (Phil. 1:9–10). They were to strive to gain the prize (1 Cor. 9:24) with continuously richer gifts of the Spirit, until the Morning Star arose in them (2 Pet. 1:19) and they were mature enough through new and greater revelations to receive the final appearance of Jesus Christ, at which time all nations would be subjected to him through the Last Judgment (Rev. 19:11–21, 20:11–15).

Growth without the Spirit

HISTORY TELLS US that after the death of the apostles, the Christians continued to preach farther and farther afield, with great zeal. They were bent on converting as many people as possible. But history also shows us that the church was not mature enough or strong enough to challenge and overcome the pagan spiritual influences introduced by the new converts. The church succumbed to the mighty blows of Greek and Roman learning and philosophy. The result of the Christians' battle to convert the nations was the formation of a church patterned on Roman statesmanship. Since they received no further revelations, they had no other model for the establishment of the church of God than the state institutions. According to the model of a state, the church was set up with rulers and subjects, lords and servants, high and low ranks, clergy and laymen. Thus the church of Jesus Christ anchored itself on worldly principles that constantly choked the divine principles given in Christ. Even to this day, we don't know how to establish a church of God in the spirit of Christ – we are perplexed and powerless. Even God's free gospel has become dependent on state and secular authorities.

I am convinced that the *first* grace and revelation, which enabled the disciples to proclaim the gospel, cannot be the *last* grace and revelation. After preaching the word and working miracles, which were necessary in the early days to establish churches, even more disclosure of the life of Christ was meant to follow.[4] Churches were not only to be planted, but in time they

---

4 Christoph Blumhardt took seriously the idea that God spoke his final word in Jesus Christ (Heb. 1:1–2). But it was just as important for Blumhardt that God leads his church today through his Holy Spirit and reveals his will to us both through the Bible and through this clear daily guidance.

were also to receive divine guidelines, which would have given them power over all the kingdoms of the world. God's Zion was to tower above all the mountains of the world – so that all nations would see it and could be invited. But the church could not reach this height through the first outpouring of the Holy Spirit, which gave the disciples only the authority to preach. Of course they did receive further assignments, gifts, and graces (1 Cor. 1:4–8), but in blind zeal the disciples did not listen to them or discounted them. If they had listened together to the voice of their commander in chief – as the apostle John tried to do for the seven churches (Rev. 2:1–3:22) – then his call of command might well have been heard in time: "Preaching and working miracles is not your final goal. You should be going forward to receive greater revelations of my life and my glory as it is now prepared in heaven. Not you, but I myself will fill the whole universe with my glory" (Eph. 4:9–16, 4:23–24; Col. 3:1–17). Yet this voice died away, and we were left with only human preaching for all later times. Further revelations for the inner and outer building up of the church failed to appear.

But what is the good of constantly preaching without constantly receiving new revelations? Thereby we slowly create a beautiful human edifice, with no life and no movement. Even if new forms of oratory stimulate and entertain us, the real cause gets stuck or even regresses, as we see in history. By sheer preaching, without being guided by new revelations, we can even totally destroy the revelations we have already received. Therefore, we must admit that if we have no revelation, then our preaching is not the gospel anymore. Instead it is nothing but religious oratory, espousing human systems. And beware: when we cater to what is human, what is divine withdraws. Even the apostles were beset by all-too-human incidents. Already among them, we see questions, doubts, unpleasant disputes, and even quarrels of all sorts that would not have been possible if they had let themselves be governed directly by God or if they had given the Holy Spirit unrestricted power.

Listening Again and Again

IT IS BAD WHEN AN OFFICER shouts to his soldiers an order he has just received from his commander in chief so loudly and for so long that neither he nor the soldiers can hear their commander's second and third commands. They might hear the fourth command, but it does not fit the first one anymore, since the commands in between were not carried out. Confusion ensues. Then the commander in chief would rather be perfectly silent and let the officers and soldiers do as they please. This is what happened in the early days. The apostles were so intent on saving the Jews that they started too late on the Gentiles and other nations. And the apostles were so intent on preaching and performing miracles that they forgot to pay attention to new revelations. So we can see why their commander in chief's instructions became fewer and more difficult to hear. Then the apostles had to go through increasing trouble and difficulty. Most of them met a grim death, which could not be transfigured (like the death of their Master) by a life-giving act of God the Father in heaven – by the personal testimony of the one whom they had preached, namely Jesus, the resurrected one.

The Nemesis of Human Systems

SO WE CAN UNDERSTAND why after the death of the apostles the whole cause became more and more detached from the spirit of God and more and more human. The Christians clung tenaciously to Jerusalem, but after it was destroyed, both the city and the nation [in AD 70], Christianity itself appears to have been pushed toward certain judgment. On this route, the grace of God's first testimony in Christ was preserved in a few Christians where it continued to work (I almost want to say: continued to weep), but *further* revelations of the resurrected one were not forthcoming.

One last message from Jesus Christ shines into the encroaching gloom – the Revelation to John. This ominous, harrowing message from the apostle John to the seven churches (Rev. 2–3), although already shrouded in darkness, was still a call to battle. But the seven churches also disappeared, and then *Christ's* realm became the *Christians'* realm. Within this realm – this religion – innumerable human systems collide in hopeless confusion, pursuing thousands of different spiritual directions and religious schemes with their many sects and denominations. But God is anything but a system, let alone a human system. Wherever people have made religion into a system, this religion is far from God no matter how close it was to God at the beginning, yes, even if it originated from him. For to worship and then create a religious system out of this worship is just as irreconcilable as to serve a master and then assault him!

The Harm of Human Zeal

IF YOU WANT TO SEE the consequences of a drive for results, look at the development of Christianity. The more perfected the systems became, the more fragmented was the spiritual state of the believers and the greater their estrangement from God. What grim scenes – anything but divine – have unfolded as Christendom went its own way, developing in the course of time increasingly sophisticated systems, right up to the present! Anyone who still feels for God, who is honest, will not be able to keep silent about this any longer. We should be weeping bitter tears to think that the earth has been saturated with blood by Christian nations, that the Creator has been dishonored in his creatures, and that everyone goes about thinking of himself and not of what Jesus Christ wants. And all this has been done in the name of that initial command, "Go into all the world and preach the gospel to all creation" (Mark 16:15). Obsessed by this one command, Christians zealously worked on the nations for so long that the palm frond of peace turned into a sword – a sword for murdering whole nations; a sword in the hands of those who proclaim Jesus, the resurrected one, the Prince of Peace and of life! Christians should be heralding the Prince of Peace to a humankind tortured to death, and to all creation.

All workers in God's kingdom are in danger of falling into blind zeal; this can cause more harm than lazy idleness. Anyone who wants to be a worker has to remain very flexible in the hands of God, so that he can serve God in one way today and in another way tomorrow, because a new time may require new assignments. No one should be like the ox at a treadmill that walks around continuously in the same circle until he collapses and dies. The same ox that turns the mill today may have to plow tomorrow and bring in grain the day after that. But if he is not willing to be taken away from his first job, he is of no value to his master in spite of his zeal.

Here's another example. A master orders his servant to mow a field of grass. The servant works hard and mows thoroughly. After the grass is cut, he also mows the field of green wheat, which is growing next to the grass. When the foreman comes, he says: "What are you doing? Do you want to ruin our master's crops by cutting down the unripe grain?" But the servant shouts back: "By no means! The master ordered me to mow, and I am going to obey the master more than you!" So he continues to mow. When the field of wheat is finished, he mows down a field of potatoes. In the end he attacks the woods, where his scythe gets ruined and he himself collapses from working so hard. Did this servant in all his "obedience" and "zeal" help or hinder his master? Unfortunately there are many servants in God's kingdom about whom our heavenly Father must shake his head and wonder, "Shall I pity them or punish them?" So let us do our best to be sensible and useful servants, who are neither headstrong nor deaf in zealously fulfilling our current task, and who remain flexible and listen for new tasks, as often as the Master calls.

To return to our main theme, I would like to point out that as time passed, people were so badly blinded that they lost the straight path toward the goal they were on originally and strayed far away. So God had to send them on a new route, a detour, to bring them to the goal. Our first concern now is not to insist on the apostolic, but to yield to whatever God uses to lead us away from our wrong ways and bring us closer to the goal. On the foundation of Christ (which no one can remove) and on the foundation of the apostles and prophets (who are Christ's witnesses) so many human fallacies – houses of straw and wood – have been erected that God has repeatedly had to introduce new incentives to prevent human errors from choking the actual foundation of salvation and making it ineffective. The corruption of the church was often so great that sincere people from all nations felt like crying out. People cried out for truth, for reform in both the leaders and the members, and each time God heard this outcry. Finally, even though the people had taken wrong paths, he led them to that station where, to a certain degree, a victory for the pure gospel took place.

Beyond the Reformation

WHAT A BLESSING THIS STATION, the Reformation, was! But we cannot withhold the fact that what came from God was again choked out by human considerations. To this very day many people are so enamored by this particular station that they don't look for anything more. The Reformation, however, cannot be the final goal of God for the earth – the place where we are to settle down and sup on fine delicacies. I will not elaborate, for I do not want to judge, but I will simply point out that all people are called to freedom in Christ, and that this freedom should give us the ability to respond immediately when new commands herald an advance.

One look into the history of the Reformation shows that it was not meant to be a resting place for all time. Its purpose was to create a new state of affairs, in which people were given the freedom to continue seeking for [new] revelations of God's kingdom. Due to false pursuits – just like in the old church, which constantly sought to settle down in the status quo – here again people looked for the so-called pure doctrine. People thought a pure doctrine would bring peace to the nations. But this principle had the devitalizing result that everyone could think that he – and not the other person – had the pure doctrine. This produced strife and jealousy from day one. In the various areas in which the Reformation won victories, believers thought the recently validated doctrine had to be imposed on other people by force.

This is why Protestant churches and sects are strewn about like so many pieces of an exploded bomb! It is because each part is trying to sustain itself. The biggest gain – which was the *freedom* God wanted to give [his people] to continue to develop under the dawning light of Jesus Christ – was smothered in many circles in their rush to organize and secure particular churches and congregations. In the succeeding times, therefore, many spirit-filled men, who were rooted in the ground of the Reformation's freedom – a freedom which could not be eradicated anymore – developed more or less in opposition to their church. Exactly that which God had worked to his advantage in the Reformation – a Christian way of life free of human constraint – was recognized by only a few up to the present day. Still, this free way of life (even though other spirits who do not respect God may temporarily scurry about in it) is the only opening for God to send servants and prophets who can advance the kingdom of God. I thank God that the ground of freedom that was gained has so far not been destroyed, even though it was often in danger of being destroyed. I thank God, not because I am wishing for human freedom of the flesh, but because I desire freedom for God's Spirit to give new revelations on earth, revelations that will advance God's kingdom.

God's Cause Advances

UP TO A CERTAIN DEGREE this has happened. Through severe judgments the Protestant church, despite its fragmentation, repeatedly was the soil from which men of God gave witness to truth. This occurred in various places and under various circumstances, often, I admit, in opposition to prevailing church opinion. Still, it was in this manner that a measure of truth was preserved through the work of extraordinary men of God. Many different directions developed in various countries, as God saw fit to send witnesses, who gained influence. But each time it was a mistake when parties and sects championed a newly revealed truth so strongly that it again became a false system, with a tendency to take over. We mention only one example from the history of the German Protestant church: the appearance of Pietism. In Pietism, this truth shines out: that an individual can be given life with God in Christ. This truth has been preserved and can never be destroyed.

My father's life blossomed because he let himself be guided by an inner leading from God, which directed him forward. He united within himself two currents that both had their origins in the Reformation: on one hand the love for an obviously developing church that preserved itself through inherited forms and doctrines, and on the other hand the zeal and freedom that allow someone to develop their own special individuality according to the way God is leading them. He came to Möttlingen as such a personality and experienced God's leading there, which allowed him to become a man of forward movement, as I have described him above, even though he remained externally an obedient man of the church. For me the experience at Möttlingen became, so to speak, a station. My attitude toward God and God's kingdom has been and always will be directed by my father's faith – he expected new directions for God's new developments.

Pressing toward the Goal

THE MOVEMENT AT MÖTTLINGEN may seem small to many, because it did not play a big part on the great stage of the visible world. But for me, the light that shone in this movement was all the more intense. It opened up new points of view to me and many others. For this light showed something of the vastness of God's world-embracing love and mercy. And because it was a real light, from which new rays came to us in uninterrupted succession, it gave us the indestructible certainty that Jesus is alive and that he wants to testify that he lives in our day. All nations on earth must open themselves up – everyone must help – so that the globe becomes a tiny, united whole in the hand of the Creator, waiting for the time when the shout "Jesus is victor!" (which we have heard)[5] can sound forth among all nations. It is a proclamation that appears in the clouds to our international human community. Heaven and earth give witness that we have all reason to expect an advance for humankind.[6] This forward movement is awaited by different people in different ways, according to their own wishes and goals, but those who have set their sights on God's kingdom expect forward movement through revelations of God in Christ. For it is Christ alone who can plant that life which can bring about a change in people because it is eternal truth. Then God's plan of salvation can be completed in them, in order that a world, guilty with sin, may be brought back by his priestly hands to the loving heart of his Father and their Creator through his reconciling blood.

This assurance, gained through holy experiences, became, as I mentioned already, a station for me, from which I could see with holy awe

---

5   This shout, heard during Christmas 1843, marked the end of the battle to set the Dittus siblings free. See Zündel, 150–152.

6   The following sentence makes it clear that by "progress" or "advance" Christoph Blumhardt is not talking about an earthly force or a human initiative. Compare chapter 12, where he describes the same as "works of God."

that the goal was close in spite of all intervening obstacles. This glimpse kept spurring me on, so that I did not get stuck at that station. One day, when we are all at the goal, the various revelations of God that took place in obscurity will come to light. Then we will look back gratefully on one or the other memorable station that God gave. Möttlingen may well be one of those – a station that many contemporaries did not consider worth noting.

I do not know how many more stations we will have to pass through before we arrive at the goal – neither do I need to know. It is enough that Möttlingen was a station for me, and that I am hurrying on toward the goal. I have to admit that today the route is going around a sharp corner. Contradictions arise, and I have to do justice to new surroundings and new relationships. It just is a fact that Möttlingen – or the work at Bad Boll, which developed through Möttlingen – no longer matters to me. Nor does my father's work count for me now, but only whatever will bring us closer to the goal. I actually had to turn my back on Möttlingen in order to advance. But nobody should get the idea that I consider Möttlingen of little importance. Any station that we have passed through remains valuable in reaching the goal, even though the station itself has been left behind. Nobody should say that I think little of the work and battles of my father, even if I have to work and fight today in an entirely different way than he did. Yes, even if it often looks as if I were doing the opposite of what he did!

To use a picture: my father had to pull up weeds in the harvest field and tie the sheaves, but we have to dig over the old field with a spade and break up the clods of our human nature, so that God's new seed can sprout in people. This does not mean that he who weeded and tied sheaves did wrong, nor does it mean that he who turned the earth and broke up the clods did wrong. They did not accuse each other, for both served one and the same Lord, for one and the same cause. Each one rejoiced in the work of the other, even if it was entirely different from his own, because it served the Lord. I would like to ask my readers not to adopt any other viewpoint than the above about my father, Möttlingen, and our own position today. Now I will go into more detail.

PART II

The Decisive Event

Battles Within and Without

4

The Battle in Möttlingen

MY FATHER'S WORK for God's kingdom was centered on joining the battle. Through God's leading, it became clear to him that God's kingdom and his righteousness will not come if we just sit back comfortably and wait for them. Rather we have to struggle on earth if certain obstacles to God's kingdom are going to be overcome. Of course it also became clear to him through his congregation, which had been "preached to death" (a description coined by his predecessor at Möttlingen, Dr. Christian Gottlob Barth, 1799–1882), that a merely human struggle using human means would not suffice. Rather, for such a battle any person is serviceable but only as a tool of Jesus Christ's spirit.

In my father's distress at seeing truth slandered by witchcraft, he called on the name of Jesus in an unforgettable moment – a moment when he saw himself surrounded by superstition and miserable, mind-perverting, demonic, evil spirits. And it was as if lightning struck through him and filled him with fire, which from then on continued to burn in a battle against all hidden, prowling satanic beings. From that moment on, his life was warfare. The spirit of Jesus Christ within him fought against Satan and the whole of his dominion. It was not my father who fought; it was the spirit of Jesus Christ who used him as a tool on earth. Through this battle, waged by God's spirit within him, a new path opened up, on which light shone and gave new insights. Suddenly the kingdom of God was no longer religion, but history [that is, a reality on earth].

It does not matter to me now whether or not my father helped to some extent with his human gifts in the history that was unfolding and didn't depend solely on Christ's spirit to work; whether or not he made mistakes. I do wholeheartedly agree that a struggle was vital – a struggle through which God emerged again as a living being to be reckoned with. God received the focus, not humanity with its evil intentions and guilt. In such a struggle Jesus is not simply the starting point of a spiritual ascent to God, but he suddenly enters into the foreground as a living person who makes a difference for those with whom he is united. Therefore, what my father experienced in this respect is (and remains for us who later were to experience it with him) a holy victory from which we draw light and clarity. We will not relinquish this victory, even though we are no longer in the position today to talk much about it, since such a struggle against invisible obstacles to God's kingdom is not in the foreground at the moment.

A New Battle Ensues

INSTEAD I WANT TO MENTION right away that I have learned to distinguish between what was done by the spirit of Jesus Christ and what tried to creep in through my father's human zeal – which was less valuable, even disastrous. It is understandable (because it is typical of all so-called Christian activity) that my father also thought he could take matters into his own hands and zealously bring things to a conclusion. Therefore, entangled situations and incidents occurred here and there which should not have happened, when certain contacts with darkness were drawn out instead of being cut off immediately.

This more human side of the struggle led later on to the other mistake: that in his defense my father was too explicit.[1] So the holy experience could not be presented as holy to the public, and my father felt he had to try to explain this or that demonic phenomena to his friends. His friends then told others and things became public that should never have been publicized.

I tell you openly that from my vantage point today, I would rather, for God's sake, that certain experiences had never been narrated and thereby perpetuated. Much that was only of temporary importance to my father was passed on to others who had no discretion. Anyway, only half of the story could be told, and that half required a belief in transient demonic manifestations. We should occupy ourselves with this belief only if it is for God's sake. Much of what was told could be understood only by someone who had experienced it, and this got into the hands of people who, even if they approached it with the best of intentions, would not be able to make any sense of it.

---

1 For example, Johann Christoph Blumhardt, *Der Kampf in Möttlingen*, I, 2, 29–56; Zündel, 117–120, 379–382.

So, on the one hand this created a lot of useless dissension that did not bear good fruit, while on the other hand it stimulated a curiosity that could never be satisfied. Not everything experienced in such a struggle, which extends into invisible areas of human life, can be described in a way that will be understood. Also, many experiences are in no way given in order to be passed on to others. For experiences of God's kingdom, the main point is not that other people know about it, but that others may live from the fruits of what individuals in God's kingdom have experienced. I am sure Jesus and his apostles, as well as the prophets in the Old Covenant, had quiet, inner experiences that they never described. I am convinced, and can prove it from many places in scripture, that both the apostles and the prophets had a vast knowledge of the invisible world – the human and demonic influences as well as the divine. This knowledge made up the backdrop for their "theology," if I may call it that. But they did not often give us any insight into this backdrop. They may have thought, "If someone else is called again into battle, we do not need to tell them anything. They will be able to see for themselves what it looks like where the human eye is not usually permitted to see." Today if someone travels to foreign countries, it does not help them much to read many books about those countries beforehand. What they experience for themselves is what teaches them lessons indispensable for future achievements.

No Victory without a Fight

LIKEWISE, MY FATHER EXPERIENCED as much as he needed to. But then it was a mistake, and this I say openly, that he wanted to make it understandable to others who were in no way called to understand it. After all, it was the *fruit* of the experience that was most important. So it is also my concern that with our friends we unite on upholding this truth: there is absolutely no victory without a preceding struggle.

Anyone who has had anything to do with the principalities of darkness should know that such power is not toppled without a hard shaking. The strong man has to be tied up first, before his plunder can be seized and shared, as the Savior himself says (Mark 3:27). And so we also say: the congregation at Möttlingen would not have been receptive to God's kingdom the way it was for my father if he had not been the warrior who struck a blow at the vulnerable spot. With the sword that God put into his hands, he was able to cut off the enemy's head.

That much we should know. But now to ask, "What did the enemy look like?" is not only an idle question but a dangerous one. While you are examining the dead enemy, his dispersed subjects can reassemble and kill you as you are bending over the fallen foe to investigate him from head to toe to find out who he was. To a certain degree this is what happened to my father. I deplore the fact that I am asked again and yet again – even today – "What did the enemy do?" or "What does the enemy do?" I am not going to say a single word about that! I do not want to give that much importance to the devil – only to our dear God. We should take notice of people – not demons. We should fill our hearts and minds with stories of life – not death.

At this point I would like to ask forgiveness in the name of my father that images were flung into the world that could not be *fully* described, because God does not want them revealed. My father even had to first try to remember what had happened before he could describe his experiences to others. If he had let the events pass by as battles and rather held fast to the fact that life had gained the victory, then the ugly spectacle would have faded away and not been preserved along with the revitalizing divine experiences. People noticed that in our circles the peace of abiding in the light that comes from living in Jesus Christ was often deeply disturbed. As far as this concerned our own circle, we could try to correct it or dispel it. Certainly, the life of my father seen as a whole is a witness to something other than demons, as anyone could see who got to know him personally.

Growing Antagonism

IN OTHER CIRCLES, HOWEVER, where the matter was discussed without further contact with the man who had experienced it, an antagonism built up against what was published. This cast doubt on the fight itself and whether the fight had even been necessary. My father, aware of this antagonism, felt he had to refuse to answer certain questions. He was so reticent that the myth spread that he later said that he must have been mistaken. I contradict this myth categorically on the basis of my personal experiences. But this much I will admit: many of my father's musings about demonic and satanic beings and their activities at least in part may not be true, since God himself did not want to shed any light on the subject. Therefore, in typical human fashion, people gave more thought to certain experiences than these deserved.

When the struggle was made public, it had embarrassing consequences, because of a certain lack of discretion in regards to the person in whom the demons had revealed themselves – Gottliebin Dittus is mentioned frequently by my father in his history of the struggle. She could be blamed, and frequently was, for what people thought was a swindle to which my father had fallen prey. We children grew up in the presence of this spiritually powerful person.[2] I have said so before, and I will say it here again, that through her pure and natural spirit, lit by vibrant truth, we were spurred on toward the kingdom of God. The spirit that resided in her (though she was despised by many) still moves us – if we are flexible enough to strip ourselves of former opinions and traditions. I am pained that Gottliebin was discredited as long as she lived and even to this day, just because my father felt compelled to publicize incidents from her life. I hope to God that I will live to see her reputation cleared – but that will take the working of the Savior to bring truth and righteousness into our lives. Then an unjust accusation will no longer fall on someone whom we should regard only with the highest respect. A warrior such as our late sister Gottliebin, who fought alongside my father and others, will not remain buried in demonic filth forever, because it is not about her justification, but about a witness to the Savior himself, who worked in her.

The Ongoing Fight

LET PEOPLE IN OTHER CIRCLES think what they like; we have been engaged in a fight for God's kingdom ever since those days. Other sincere Christians are fighting, too, maybe in other ways, but they also realize that the kingdom of God requires soldiers ready to surrender their whole lives in whatever way they are commanded (Matt. 10:39, 16:24–25), so that they may win the crown of life (2 Tim. 2:3–5). Other people also experience that the human being is thrust into a struggle, unlike an animal that is bounded by its set nature and instincts.

Nobody would see the need for a plant or an animal to change its natural instincts. Most every living thing is to a certain degree fully developed – except the human being. Of all creatures, humans – the most advanced of all living organisms – are incomplete! If you look closely, you will discover the reason: they lack harmony between their inner and outer self, between spirit and body. The true human, humanity as created in the image of God, does not emerge. Sometimes our physical body harms our spirit, and sometimes it is the other way around, our spiritual moods harm our physical body. Then untruthfulness is generated in the physical life and in the inner life of the spirit. Compare that to plants and animals where

---

2 In 1855 Gottliebin Dittus (1815–1872) married Theodor Broderson (1829–1912), Johann Christoph Blumhardt's business manager at Bad Boll. For the Dittus family history see Johann Christoph Blumhardt, *Der Kampf in Möttlingen*, I, 2, 24–29.

the visible and invisible work together harmoniously to produce a perfect picture in the visible world. The body grows along with the impulses of life to create a perfect harmonious whole. A plant grows the way it is supposed to. But with the human creature, every individual senses something depressing in human life because our higher awareness of self is bound to be dissatisfied with the way our life is developing. The apostle Paul says, "For what I want to do I do not do, but what I hate I do" (Rom. 7:15). The entire human race can endorse Paul's statement to some extent.

Most people, when they realize what state they are in, look for perfection only for their own personal lives. But people of God, who wait for his kingdom, try to draw on God's perfection for the whole of human life, and this is the meaning of Christ in the world. In him, through God's mercy, God wants to plant a perfect humanity into the world in contrast to an only relatively perfect or even totally imperfect humanity, so that now all people who believe in Jesus may expect the coming of a perfect creation – God's goodness, truth, and justice in perfect form (Matt. 5:48). But in this expectation they cannot just be inactive spectators, waiting to see how and when God will intervene and miraculously drop the perfect out of the sky to take the place of the imperfect. No, the effect of Jesus Christ's coming into the world is that all those who believe in him, by his grace, now feel continuously driven to grow toward perfection and to put on the new nature, which lives in true righteousness and holiness (Eph. 4:24; Col. 3:12ff.). This persistent drive is like perpetual motion; it is like a power source that turns the gears, enabling the believer to achieve feats superior to the usual achievements of men and women. The achievements of apostles and prophets – and that is basically what all those who believe in Jesus are – are far superior to the achievements of other people, because they allow the invisible God to have his rightful place in their inner being, and make room for his glory and his discernment.

The Need for Vanguards

INASMUCH AS THIS DRIVE for God's will provokes resistance in our existing world, there will be conflict. This battle has to start in our inner life. We must believe that if we clean up our inner lives, cleansing them of all sorts of obstacles, then our visible lives will display a clear and true life. Actually, all people are called to take up this battle, because no one *wants* to be bad. But only a few are chosen; most people are not willing to submit to the narrow path of faith in Jesus, which means dying to their own flesh – or they just cannot understand this path.

Therefore, there must be vanguards – fighters who experience victories on behalf of many, sometimes against spiritual obstacles (taken as a whole we can call them "the powers of darkness"), sometimes against obstacles that rest in our physical bodies (for these I would like to use the term "the flesh"). I am convinced that the flesh can be overcome only to the extent to which the power of darkness has been broken beforehand. Yes, a struggle for truth in the physical body comes about all by itself, according to the degree that our inner impulses can move freely, delivered from false influences. In other words, the physical life, as it manifests itself on earth, can take on a true and eternal form only insofar as the inner life has become true and eternal.

That this is so is shown in the lives of those whose struggles are recorded in scripture. They all battled against things in themselves and in their surroundings that were foreign to the truth and to a godly life. The spirit of God fights against the spirit of the world. John's Revelation clearly states that we must at least admit that foreign spirits have entered into humanity and that this was not God's original intention. It is part of God's will only in this respect: God appointed humanity to fight against this foreign spirit, against evil, against what in the course of history has come to be called "demonic," or, at its peak, "satanic." When men and women of God win a battle for truth against this unjust and lying being in their inner life, then their outer life will immediately take on a new form – true and eternal (as far as the eternal is possible within time).

God's Warriors Show the Way

BECAUSE ABRAHAM, FOR EXAMPLE, overcame in himself the obstacles that could have tied him to the ideas of his time and his lineage, and because he decided to believe in God, his whole life changed. Then righteousness was placed within him like a seed, a divine justice and righteousness, which grew and held within itself God's justice and righteousness for the whole world. Because Jacob struggled inwardly with God and with humans and overcame (so that he was assured of God and his fellowship), he became Israel – the battle zone – and the promise for the future fell into his lap (Gen. 32:28). Because Moses overcame the darkness that inwardly enshrouded him and gave himself to God (so that God spoke his words of righteousness and truth to him), the victory over Egypt was given and Israel was saved from the angel of wrath who went throughout all of Egypt. But even though the people of Israel were freed from the yoke of Egypt by the mighty hand of God that fought and won through Moses, and were well cared for in the desert, it was of no help to them because they did not personally take up the inner battle against evil. They took the Egyptian demons with them into the desert. The people looked more to these demons than to the angels of God and his spirit, so they soon craved to be back in Egypt. Only a few took up the inner battle and remained alive – the others died in the desert. The entire history of Israel was fruitful for God's kingdom only insofar as individuals took up the right position in this internal battle. If someone acknowledged God, then he was a prophet and wrought signs and wonders. If someone acknowledged the nations and their demons, then he became a destroyer of the people; he took on the form of a demon.

Obviously, "the flesh desires what is contrary to the Spirit, and the Spirit what is contrary to the flesh" (Gal. 5:17). Because most people sow to please their flesh (Gal. 6:7–8) – that is, their current desires, where pleasure rules – they follow what they themselves want and thereby come under the power of false spirits called demons. The prophets of Israel, possessed by God's spirit, took on the inner battle against these false spiritual powers again and again and gained victories for truth for themselves and for those who recognized the prophets as warriors of God. So whoever turned himself over to God inwardly was saved outwardly, even during the darkest and most fateful times in Israel's history.

God's Son Gains the Victory

IT WENT ON LIKE THIS until Christ. His life, too, was an uninterrupted struggle for God and for the true life that comes from God. We can certainly assume that Christ struggled from the time he could walk. He was the real, true Israel. His every breath was a fervent prayer for God to come on earth: "God in heaven" – he calls him Father – "hallowed be *your* name! *Your* kingdom and dominion come! *Your* will be done *on earth*!" This is what Jesus came for: *to establish God's justice on earth.* Inwardly stronger than all of his forerunners, unmistakably and personally one with God himself, he was the true God and the eternal life, a warrior against anything that was not of God, whether it was within human beings or outside of them. For a kingdom of Satan had come into being that sought control over God's creation and carried on its work outside of human beings. A great internal victory against this kingdom prepared the way for Jesus and his public ministry.

John the Baptist could appear only on the basis of Jesus' battles, as he said himself: "A man who comes after me has surpassed me because he *was before me*" (John 1:30), and that is why he found that all the people were prepared to repent and be baptized for the forgiveness of their sins and to wait for the kingdom of God. It is true that nothing is told us specifically about the struggle that paved the way, but we can see it in the people who felt themselves captivated by this fighting spirit and who then followed John the Baptist and later on Jesus of Nazareth, in order to equip themselves for God's kingdom. The victory won by John the Baptist was not complete. It succeeded only insofar as the people of Israel felt the freedom to separate themselves from the conventional temple worship services, to the extent that they did not look for forgiveness of sin in the temple but with the man in the desert. This prepared for the fulfillment of the words, "God is spirit, and his worshipers must worship him in spirit and in truth" (John 4:24). Traditional forms of worship were about to fall away.

But for Jesus it was important to fight for more than that. His inner struggle is obvious in everything he says and does, and the Gospels give plenty of indications of this. In regards to his own person, there was also a mighty battle with Satan (Matt. 4:1–11). In this struggle a personal being is seen clearly for the first time, with whom Jesus enters into battle. In that being, the world detached from God steps into the foreground with its own spirit. Though God may be acknowledged, he is not wanted. Human beings, under the influence of the prince of this world, think they should be independent and create their fortunes on their own steam. That is why this spiritual being is called Satan, which means "enemy of God." In Jesus the opposite is true – God alone steps into the foreground. Jesus claims God's supreme authority and wins the victory in the fight for God's authority in his own person – so successfully that angels came to serve him (Mark 1:13) and what the voice of God had said was confirmed: "You are my Son, whom I love; with you I am well pleased" (Matt. 3:17). This struggle, which ended with a glorious victory, had to come first, before Jesus could rise again and assert God's right to his people. An inner victory had to be won first, before Jesus could dare to make a public appearance with any prospect of success.

More Battles to Be Fought

BUT STILL THE BATTLE was not over. The whole rest of Jesus' life among his people tells of continuous inner wrestling with the repulsive and lying character who opposed life and who had gained dominion over human beings. Israel was virtually no longer the people of God in the true sense. As a whole it had actually never been a people of God, an Israel according to the spirit (cf. Rom. 2:28–29, 9:6). Only in hope was Israel spared until Christ came (Gal. 3:24). Rather, Israel was in the grip of God-opposing spiritual powers, to which people in their selfishness gave homage, just as Christ himself said: "You belong to your father, the devil, and you want to carry out your father's desires" (John 8:44). Due to this the members of the nation of Israel, though they worshiped the living God outwardly, were still in the same sorrows of death as the rest of humankind. People did not feel any trace of eternal life, and God also received no testimony from his people. But now Jesus, God's witness, appears and with him eternal life. This is connected to the fact that he alone brings God's justice on earth. Now he fights on behalf of his brethren, first of all for the lost sheep of the house of Israel (Matt. 10:5–6, 15:24), but in spirit he already draws all lost people into the realm of his battle (Matt. 28:19).

If we take a closer look, we can see that Jesus wages a *two-fold battle* for God on earth. What human beings could not do, God did through the name of Jesus. On one side, Jesus, in the Spirit, fought against the purely *demonic* – the invisible kingdom of Satan that entangles humanity. Step by step he became Lord over this invisible domain. The deliverance of people who were chained in Satan's fetters was part of this fight. This is why the Gospels tell so often about demons.

But the deliverance of individual people from demons, even the fact that Jesus in his person could overcome any satanic being, did not eliminate the other, further battle, namely the one *within humanity*. This struggle is also at first an inner one. The question is whether people who are freed from the demonic are willing to yield their inner being to God, just as Jesus sacrificed himself solely for God, and lived for God's truth and justice.

This last battle was the toughest one and ended at first in what seemed to be a defeat. As it says: "This is the verdict: light has come into the world, but people loved darkness instead of light" (John 3:19). The inner being of humanity was not won over, and the brighter the victory for God shone in the person of Jesus Christ, the more the flesh rose up against this victory and human beings were filled anew with darkness. The result was the horrible murder of the Lord Jesus, the most atrocious work of the flesh, which wars against the spirit.

But Jesus, the Lord, did not lose the victory, because he knew how to surrender not only his inner self but also his body to God. He handed over his body to be transfigured, and decay had no power over him. Freed from the death of the body, he comes forth from the grave. Having risen from the dead, he gathers his disciples not to be an external religious community with outward laws and doctrines but to be fellow fighters in the battle that he – as the one who has risen from the dead – now wants to wage more than ever against Satan's powers on the one side and against the flesh on the other side. In this battle he will recreate the whole of humanity, by establishing the authority of God in man.

Where the Battle Continues

THE APOSTLES AND ALL DISCIPLES of Jesus, those who come into contact with the resurrected one, are in actual fact warriors, fighters in the inner regions of the human soul. On one hand demonic authorities and powers that we cannot see or understand wreak their havoc in our inner beings, and on the other hand our own human nature – which in scripture is called the flesh – obstinately turns away from God. That is why throughout apostolic history there are references to struggle. First of all, we are fighting "not against flesh and blood, but against the rulers, against the authorities, against the powers of this dark world and against the spiritual forces of evil in the heavenly realms" (Eph. 6:12), but at the same time we are fighting against sin and the flesh, which so easily hinders and entangles us (Heb. 12:1). It is a battle for God within human beings, a battle for the faith that will enable us to work for God and for his justice and his kingdom.

What shape and form this inner battle took for the apostles cannot be traced in detail, because they gave us only a few isolated indications of it. We cannot watch such an inner battle the way we can see an external conflict between nations. The overall picture of the battle escapes even the warriors themselves. Because they themselves are visible beings and because they rely on what they can see, they are not able to completely comprehend the invisible enemy opposing them. It is also none of their concern to give to visible human beings a history of the invisible world, to explain or elucidate the history of Satan and his angels. However, they certainly are called to show their mettle when they meet any resistance to God – whether this resistance comes from Satan's realm or whether it originates from the flesh and is a human resistance – and to prove themselves to be reliable soldiers of God. They must be men and women for whom nothing counts except the rule of God in the world and who are one hundred percent focused on their goal that Jesus must become Lord on earth and in heaven and under the earth (cf. Matt. 28:18; Phil. 2:10).

Putting On the Armor of God

THEREFORE, THEY DO NOT NEED to think about the appearances of principalities and powers, of demons and demonic apparitions. They only need to know that there is in fact another world besides the world of living human beings and that this other world is opposed to God and bent on drawing men and women into its spell. Anyways, they are only warriors in individual combat, similar to soldiers who do not need to have an overview of the enemies' hosts – it is enough that the commander in chief tells them when and where they should fight. Whether they are led by the great commander in chief to fight against invisible enemies in the satanic realm at one time or to fight against invisible urges of the flesh at another time, in both cases the *battle position* must be sustained. A disciple of Jesus is in essence a soldier, and his life is a story of inner struggle. He strives ceaselessly toward the great goal of God's kingdom and becomes more and more radiant as he goes through these experiences. The end of *this* story is the crown of life (Rev. 2:10) or God crowning his creation by giving back the Sabbath.

The victory over the outer, visible obstacles to God's kingdom should follow as a result of this history of inner struggling. Every single religious or secular practice, custom, or folkway has either emerged from the flesh or is at least contaminated by the flesh.[3] That is why they hinder true life on earth. And that is why they have to be abolished to make room for God's perfect plan and his perfect order. The Gentiles and all nations will come to Zion, the embodiment of God's order for life, when the time is fulfilled, that is, when the inner struggle has been completed by the people of God. But we people will not fully understand the implications of this struggle, which has now been going on for centuries, until this Zion, which is still hidden in Christ with God, appears publicly at the return of Jesus Christ, the resurrected one.

We can only say this much: after the time of the apostles this battle receded as far as being a priority of the *church*. Certainly, some individuals never entirely stopped fighting, but we get the impression that advocates of Christianity were more intent on spreading the outward form of Christendom than on triumphing over the inner obstacles to the kingdom of God latent in humankind.

That is how Christendom developed into a world power on the one hand, and on the other hand demonic powers entered again and the flesh also continued to wreak havoc unhindered. Christendom was marred for the greater part by human and demonic elements, and to be a "Christian"

---

3 Christoph Blumhardt uses the expression "flesh" (as the apostle Paul did) to describe the human capabilities that we have at our disposal. To the extent that our own abilities make us depend on ourselves and not rely solely on God, our "flesh" is an obstacle to our faith. Blumhardt increasingly emphasized that it is precisely our piety which can become "flesh": by our own efforts we can look pious, but we are actually relying on ourselves and not on God.

was no longer a guarantee that you were not the devil incarnate, seizing power within the church of Christ. Thereby the flesh gained superiority over the spirit, and Christ was, so to speak, *crucified again*. He, Christ, could no longer manifest himself as the resurrected one on earth.

Where the Reformation Stalled

THERE HAVE PROBABLY ALWAYS been some currents of people who have resisted this second murder of Jesus, the resurrected one – people who have resisted a corpulent Christendom that caters to people's cravings. We owe a lot to one such countercurrent, the Reformation – not to mention other countercurrents. For Luther (and for the other Reformers), the inner struggle clearly took center stage ahead of outer considerations – even if we cannot see it as clearly in their case as we can with the apostles. If Luther would not first have become convinced in his heart of hearts of the power of God in the battle against Satan and against human accomplishments, if he would not first have become a firm advocate for the truth of God, his public stand against the errors of the church would have had just as little success as the public protests of others in whom the victory was not as complete. But on the other hand it also has to be said that the Reformers did not overcome many ambiguities and works of the flesh related to their time, so the truth did not fully break through.

It is too bad (and this often happens) that the pioneers, when they had won their first victory, were so eager to take advantage of it that it did not occur to them that they still needed to go through many struggles. They would have to win many victories before they would have the authority to challenge other opinions – they didn't yet have the finished product. So the first victory failed to bring the truth to light for all of Christianity clearly enough that all resistance would crumble. Instead the process stagnated. Today, too, many claim to be in the right, but God has not given them the authority to defeat the others.

This much is certain, however: the Reformation was the basis for forward movement toward the kingdom of God. Now, for further advances, new soldiers and coworkers for God can and should come forward, not to establish a new church, but to form a community able to greet their Lord with burning lights. In the name of Jesus, warriors for God should gather who, through the light that has been set on fire in their hearts, are able to defend themselves against any interference from above or below, from the right or the left, which so easily could entice them back into serving the demons and Satan.

Jesus had come back into the foreground for millions. His presence could be felt. He came alive again, so to speak, and the many barriers put up by the old church could no longer completely take his breath away on earth. At least space was made for Jesus to live. But again the same danger threatened: people paid less attention to the inner struggles and victories for God and more attention to the expansion of the Protestant churches in their struggle against the old church. So for the Protestant churches, too, the church became more important than Jesus. Most Christians fought to spread the church's gospel. Few took up the unfinished task of winning the complete victory over Satan and the flesh and opening the way to the resurrection of Christ.

Therefore, to this very day, Jesus Christ – as the resurrected one – has rarely emerged, and then only in hidden places, not even in the Protestant churches. Nor has his second coming been made possible! On the whole, the *eternal* light shines just as little from these new Christians as it does from those in the old church.

The Protestant churches put most of their efforts into holding firmly to the outer form of their confession because of its differences with other Christian confessions. So, as time went on, they forgot that they should be continuing the inner struggle that Jesus and the apostles had started. They didn't realize that this struggle would culminate in victories for life won by Jesus Christ that would be the actual beginning of the kingdom of God on earth. Even though individual witnesses of the gospel proved themselves to be warriors, they were mostly unaware of it themselves and remained more or less tied to the peculiarities of the confession they were born into and fought for those points just as hard as for the kingdom of God. So those who fought for their church or for their souls thought they were fighting for the kingdom of God and did not realize that to a great extent they were making concessions both to Satan and to the flesh when it suited them.

More Ground to Conquer

MY FATHER, AS THE PASTOR of Möttlingen, was at first totally caught up in the effort to bring his church's gospel to his congregation, hoping that from this teaching faith would come forth, and from faith life, and from life the kingdom of God would be seen. He soon realized he was mistaken, and he became grieved in his spirit after he had worked for several years with his natural enthusiasm and personal conviction. Unbeknownst to him, a battle for the *kingdom of God* was slowly beginning which led beyond ordinary Christianity. He sensed the inadequacy of churchy Christendom and this prepared him to experience something extraordinary. Suddenly he was faced with a morass, issuing from the depths of a human soul – a quagmire he had never met before. Others before him knew a lot about devils and demons and could tell so much that dealings with them had become a favorite health remedy. Witchcraft was rampant in the locality, accompanied by the worst deception.

My father was convinced that no one on earth has final authority except the living God in Jesus. Now he encountered demonic entanglements and realized that for anyone involved in these, the Lord Jesus' right to their hearts had been taken away, even if they knew the truth of the gospel. When my father saw with his inner eye whole areas within human beings engulfed by satanic powers, he did not confer with any human being. Unlike all his friends, he launched into the struggle for God – the struggle handed down to us by the apostles and prophets. It is not surprising that when he reopened this fight (which claimed his entire being) he could not foresee the scope of this battle, even though a divine light led him and gave him strength. It also should not surprise anybody who knows that human beings can become captives of Satan that in the beginning disconcerting apparitions appeared from the invisible world and affected the visible world. These apparitions were misleading, deceiving, and confusing. In spite of all this, my father was a warrior and continued to be a warrior, on the whole in the right way, even though he made mistakes. The right way was the way that impelled him to the one and only point that mattered: "Jesus is victor!" – and everything else must cease.

I have to give my father credit for not fighting for himself but for the victory of Jesus Christ and for God's rightful claim in people through Jesus Christ. He risked his life, suffered mockery and ridicule, did not despair in the face of fallacies, and did not grow weak or weary when he realized that he had made mistakes. Instead, at all times his attitude was: "Not I, but Jesus Christ must reign!" Whether anybody could understand anything in the thick of the battle or not didn't matter – the outcome would reveal everything.

5

Unintended Consequences

I HAVE ALREADY REFERRED to the difficulties that ensued after my father's publications about his experiences with the inner, emotional areas of the human being. But I want to go into more detail here. My father himself sensed that the publication could create problems, as we can see by what he wrote in the preface to the memorandum he submitted to his ecclesiastical superiors at their request. Under the title, "Account of Gottliebin Dittus's Illness" he wrote:

> In submitting the following report to the greatly esteemed high consistory of the church, I feel urged to state that until now I have not spoken to anybody about my experiences with such boldness and candor. Even my best friends look at me askance and have put me into the embarrassing position of having to keep complete silence toward them, for it is as though they felt in danger if they so much as heard about these things. At the same time, I owe them thanks for constantly trembling for me during the time of my struggle. Since by far the largest part of it has up to now remained an undisclosed secret I could have taken with me to the grave, I was completely free to select what I pleased for this report; it would have been easy for me to give an account that would not have offended any reader. That, however, I could not bring myself to do. Even though at almost every paragraph I had to ask myself with trembling if it was not rash and imprudent to tell everything just as it was, time and again an inner voice would say, "Out with it!"
>
> So I dare to do it, and I do it in the name of Jesus, who is the victor. I considered it my responsibility to be honest and frank, especially in this matter, and not only toward the highly esteemed high consistory of

the church, which has every right to expect frankness from me, but also toward my Lord Jesus, for whose cause alone I had to take up the struggle. As I speak out unreservedly for the first time, I have the understandable wish that the information given here be regarded as private, as when close friends share a secret.

There is a second request I may be permitted to make: that the esteemed readers please read the whole report several times before forming a judgment. Meanwhile I put my trust in Him who has the hearts of humanity in His power. However the verdicts may turn out, I rest assured in the knowledge of having spoken the unvarnished truth and in the rock-like certainty that Jesus is victor.[1]

An Authentic Account

MY FATHER SHEDS FURTHER LIGHT on his memorandum in his *Written Defense against Dr. de Valenti*:

Since one has long since got used to stories of demonic manifestations, particularly clairvoyance, not coming to a sensible conclusion, one could, of course, say that I should have been more prudent and left out of my report whatever might be interpreted as unbounded self-conceit. But I was well aware of all this, and people should not think I was overly honest out of sheer stupidity. If I had to give an account – and that I had been asked to do – I was not going to twist the truth by presenting the case as simply one more demonic vagary or fraud, such as have so often been seen and heard in these last decades. I would have been ashamed to be regarded as one of those adventurous freaks who so often foolishly play around with happenings and appearances from the other world. I approached the matter in question in the fear of God, and if it took on a much more serious character than any similar occurrences, I had to make that clear to my superiors – to justify myself, if for no other reason. Once I put anything in writing . . . I had to write down everything, so I related openly and unreservedly how I had reasoned and acted. In this way, too, I could all the more confidently wait for the outcome; if I was wrong or in error or conceited, my superiors should know it and be in a position to judge it. For I have no wish to set up a barricade of silent obstinacy, as certain false trends and demonic spiritual cliques do these days, where dupes scheme all sorts of things in secret and let no one who is not yet fully one of them peer into their clandestine doings. My cause was to come to the light and

---

1 Johann Christoph Blumhardt, "Krankheitsgeschichte," in *Der Kampf in Möttlingen*, I, 1, 32f. English translation taken from Zündel, 118–119.

was to be examined in the light, but of course only by my superiors and as if under a seal of confession. To them I would tell it but for the time being to no one else. And I kept my word too.[2]

These words give us an insight into the difficulties my father had because of the stand he took when he realized that many people in his congregation believed in superstitions and were involved with demons. Today, as we consider these words of his, we see above all the integrity of a childlike man, who could not bring himself to conceal anything whatsoever that had taken place within the church of Jesus Christ. My father felt himself to be a child of his church, and he perceived his church as a large family in which everyone shares with each other everything they experience. So it seemed to him dishonest to conceal experiences that had changed not only his own inner life, but everything around him so thoroughly that notice was taken of it even in far-off countries.

Biblical Testimony and Authority

MY FATHER ALSO FELT the need for open discussion about this, since biblical stories fall into the same category. We can't visualize the life of Jesus without considering the question: What were the demons from which people of those days were delivered? Why did physical healing follow as a result of being delivered? Are these stories a swindle on the part of the Lord Jesus himself and his contemporaries? Or do they conceal sparks of truth that shed light on sin and death in both nations and individuals? We have to decide – it's one or the other.

In general, my father realized that his experiences confirmed the biblical concept that people can be physically and mentally corrupted by foreign spirits or demons. Specifically, he realized that demons obstruct the kingdom of truth and righteousness just as much today as they did in Jesus' day.

My father believed he should give clear proof that the main reason for people getting involved with demons is because they are superstitious. It is not a small matter whether the Christian community agrees on these three points or not. Of course it is difficult to come to an agreement, especially since innumerable people think it is superstitious even to uphold these three points: [1] that Jesus was not mistaken, [2] that the danger of getting entangled with demons was not only real in his day but immanent in all ages, and that even today the populace submits all too easily to such

---

2 English translation from Zündel, 119–120.

temptations, and [3] that superstition and idol worship can lead people to both mental and physical harm. Many people think it is being superstitious even to recognize and oppose existing superstitions.

Now, a great injustice was done to my father, namely, that most people did not take to heart how terribly strongly his spirit protested against popular belief in superstition. He published articles to prove how important it is to attack the practice of superstition from all sides.[3] He published to awaken horror against it. He denounced it in the name of Jesus. He pleaded for people to beware of the repulsive, seductive, and benumbing work of witches, charmers, and sorcerers. He called out to the public: "What foolishness are you doing with heathen charms? Why do you try to protect your houses, your livestock, and your children with magic spells and amulets, and by choosing certain days? [Don't you realize that] you have the living God to help you?" With the watchword "Jesus is victor!" – not sin, hell, death, or the devil – he tried to bring the eternally freeing blessing to thousands and tens of thousands. But all of this was disregarded from a certain quarter, and my father was maliciously labeled as an obscure reactionary who believed in demons.

Yet he was the one who had the least faith in demons and the devil, for he counted them as nothing, since Jesus alone is the way and the truth and the life (John 14:6). It has often troubled me that exactly those people who turned their backs on my father because he believed in demons secretly cherished superstitious practices. Once when I was a child, I was a guest at the table of a Christian family. The family became very fearful when they realized that we would be thirteen people around the table for the meal. One person had to sit on the side. People like these condemned my father, even though he had freed himself, his family, and all of his friends from such foolishness.

Just a few years ago, we installed an electric calling system in one of our houses. The electrician did not even bring the number 13 with him. His numbers jumped from 12 to 14, but we had a Room 13. When we asked him why he omitted the number 13, he answered that no one permits him to install the number 13 since many people are afraid to live in a room with that number. Such a society condemned my father! We could give many examples of how even educated people were and still are caught up in such superstitions and yet they act as if they were enlightened.

---

3 Johann Christoph Blumhardt repeatedly opposed different forms of superstition. The best resource is the subject index in *Gesammelte Werke*, II: *Blätter aus Bad Boll*, vol. 5, *Erläuternder Anhang* (Göttingen: Vandenhoeck & Ruprecht, 1974), 251ff.

I give my father credit for freeing himself and his people to the core from such foolishness. Of course he talked about the dangers of superstition again and again, not because he believed in it but because so many people did not want to give it up and therefore were actually damaged in body and soul. Even though a lot of effort has been made in our day to educate people about common superstitions, it is still very important to proclaim how ridiculous and foolish superstitious notions are and how dangerous they can be for people who through this get involved in more serious entanglements. I do not hesitate to acknowledge wholeheartedly how earnest and zealous my father was in this matter, even if it might make people think I am superstitious – which I know I certainly am not!

The Failure of the Church

I DO NOT WANT to expand any further on the danger many people are in today, who pay more attention to other invisible powers – and even submit themselves to them – than to the power of God. The only thing I will say here is that my father's publications would have borne much better fruit if his readers had been ready to see how much he did not have faith in the devil and how much he did have faith in Christ, the man of truth. If my father's presupposition had been correct, that we have a church, a fellowship filled with the Holy Spirit, in which whatever happens is accepted in a brotherly way and used for the benefit of all, then it would have been correct to share everything without reserve, even matters that could provoke an argument. It was not a question of whether or not the events had happened, but a question of testing whether or not the events had lasting value or were better forgotten. But sadly, my father's presupposition was false: we did not and still do not have a fellowship filled with the Holy Spirit which can judge and purify everything so that God can use it to benefit the church of Jesus Christ. Therefore, we must reproach my father for his honesty, because it was bound to cause trouble.

It has been a mistake since early times that the church of Jesus Christ thought it had to incorporate all members of an entire people. This was not the meaning of the church when the apostles founded it. There is a difference between the church being salt among the nations (Matt. 5:13) and the nations becoming the church. If you want to make the nations into churches in the present time, then you have to set up churches in keeping with the people. But because people are still superstitious, the church has to make concessions to superstitions and allow idolatrous ideas and practices. Then the church has to forgo much truth until the people are mature enough to receive truths that can be understood only in a fellowship filled with the Holy Spirit. The nations on earth can make no sense of the revelation of God in Christ, nor can they foresee its repercussions for the individual – true freedom given to those who live toward God.

So today, too, we get into a predicament anytime we perceive something from God, simply because we cannot publish it in a circle where it belongs. Instead, we are in the embarrassing position that whatever is published gets to the church and through the church to the whole nation – to innumerable people who cannot understand it. Then, in the name of the church, people protest against it. For in the church they want to hear only what they understand and what suits them. So my father was more or less rejected, because people thought that if they associated with him they would also be seen as fools by the so-called educated Christian world – all the more so because his faith was already a jab against certain superstitious practices within the church, from which even Protestantism could not keep free.

My Father's Dilemma

MY FATHER FELT ALL THIS already when he wrote that preface. He could not help being afraid that the publication of his experiences might not be right. That's why on one side he declared courageously: "Out with it!" (that is, to the fellowship of his brothers and sisters) and on the other side he felt: "Do not come out with it!" (that is, to all the world). We see how he stood with a precipice on either side. One precipice or danger was to keep silent. For this was true: simply to withhold the truth and then act as if there were no brothers at all in the world who, by following the Holy Scriptures, could understand demonic influences would have been wrong and would have caused the most damage to my father himself. His personal inner life would have become stunted through this kind of untruthfulness. The other precipice or danger was to publish the account, because it did not reach only the right listeners, which took away much of the blessing of my father's work. In the end, the whole world got involved with his experiences, and the decisive voice in my father's condemnation came from groups that were in no way qualified to have any say about the sacred events experienced by someone who fought for God's glory. A church such as my father had presupposed simply did not exist.

The ones who gave this decisive voice were then (just as they still are today) from those circles that believe in prevailing scientific theories and that hold authority within the existing church. Certainly many people were not only delivered from their superstitious notions through my father but experienced miracles through their firm faith in Christ. But these people were slowly silenced and were surrounded by superstitious people, who made themselves heard. They appropriated my father's account to validate their belief in demons. And, of course, they added fictitious material, which to this day has not yet been eradicated.[4]

Due to these circumstances the material published in my father's account was more dangerous than he realized at the time. People focused on the lurid, demonic distortions, while they passed over the loving, friendly, divine guidance that stood by him in specific spiritual battles. Since people were used to inexplicable incidents, it was bound to happen that unqualified people began trying to drive out demons and in so doing referred to my father. These people had no idea of God's call and the clear guidance under which my father acted and without which nobody should dare to lift even a finger to tamper with things that cannot be perceived with our human senses. Granted, he also made the mistake of assuming that others would be just as childlike as he was, and so he cherished the opinion that others could fight battles like he had. But unless a person has been specifically endowed and unless they are led by the light, they will not be able to bring forth any good fruit in this realm for the benefit of God's kingdom.

However that may be, throughout my father's later ministry he connected with many thousands of people, all of whom felt him to be a most sensible man who in all simplicity lived in the visible world. That should be proof enough that his zealous battle against demonic entanglement in no way affected his soul at a deeper level. Any demonic chains lay broken under my father's feet, unworthy of further notice. Before him rose the light of God's kingdom with its truth, which lifted people out of the muddy waters of sin and death. Yet it cannot be denied that harm had been done, which slumbered in the shadows – the demonic episodes described by my father evoked a response in many superstitious people that he had never intended. In spite of all his light-filled sermons, this accusation was always lurking in the background and growling at his heels: "It's all about devils and demons after all." Mistrust like this lingers on even to the present. This situation has been aggravated, because in time unauthorized groups attained my father's account and published it, sometimes in periodicals, sometimes as a special

---

4 Even today, my father is constantly cited as a key witness for trying to legitimize a Christian's involvement with parapsychology or even used to engage spiritualistic phenomena. He separated himself clearly from all this as much as he could. But it is strange that he told Justinus Kerner of the occurrences on his own. Did he consider Kerner a specialist and wish to receive his opinion? See *Der Kampf in Möttlingen* I, 1, 29–31; 79ff. and the corresponding note; I, 2, 119–120.

edition (as happened recently in Württemberg), and sometimes with the insertion of total lies, thereby further damaging the blessed memory of my father.[5] Of course it is not the fault of these ignorant people – some of whom wanted to advance themselves by using my father's experiences to defend their own impure dealings with invisible beings. Others ridiculed the manuscript. The fault lies squarely on my father's shoulders, and I do not hesitate to admit this. For it cannot be denied that (even though it was not his intention) because of the publication of these demonic episodes what God wanted to do through this witness was cast into a false light.

Superstition and Demons Today

FROM TODAY'S PERSPECTIVE, I feel obliged to comply more fully with my father's original wishes. I therefore ask my readers to realize that it is our duty when we hear rumors of demonic apparitions – the duty of all friends of God's kingdom – to regard these episodes as he did, merely as evidence of an underlying battle. Aside from that, these external manifestations should not carry any weight for the faith of those who hope in Jesus Christ. It is not pretty when our faith in God and in his true creation is mixed with faith in ungodly spirits and demonic perversions of nature – that is, faith in superstition. Faith in superstition is all the more destructive because this kind of faith gives the natural person greater sensual pleasure. Through superstition a person can wallow in obscure fantasies and also falsely justify his own perverted nature. To mix faith in God with faith in the devil has the result, for countless people, that they think they can blame the devil for their godless behavior – a perfectly heathen idea.

My father considered it detrimental to our faith in God to want to understand demonic or satanic episodes. If we do that, the dark side of human nature plays a bigger role than the light of life, which shines in Jesus to the glory of God. Now, if, because of the publication of these demonic episodes in my father's biography, an admiration of dark things has been laid at my doorstep – so that due to circumstances against my will I am co-guilty for many people adopting this wrong interest and admiration – that is all the more reason for me to explain that now we have to fix our eyes on something altogether different from the filth which came to light in Möttlingen – filth resulting from years of superstition and occult practices. It is an unfortunate characteristic of human nature that we love to gaze at the horror of sin in the flesh and do not want to let go of it, while we belittle anything pure, simple, or divine.

---

5 See *Der Kampf in Möttlingen*, I, 2, 46, 50, 53.

In Möttlingen at that time, the house was swept clean of all its dirt and garbage and put in order, so to speak (Matt. 12:44). Instead of enjoying the clean house, people went to the garbage pile again and again and pawed through it, trying to find the dirt that had been in the house. Let us purge ourselves of this impulse. And as we do so, please don't infer that we are underestimating the significance of a man having once been called upon to cleanse the Augean stables[6] of superstition. Today we do not want to take any interest in the seamy side of life but instead turn ourselves exclusively to what moved my father from the beginning.

The Power of God's Living Word

ALREADY DURING THE SO-CALLED "STRUGGLE" the most important thing for my father was direct contact with the living Word of God. God's Word equipped him almost like a prophet. At that time he was so filled with God's Word that he spent the rest of his life striving for the light of God's revelation in Jesus the Lord. He didn't think, "Satan is great and strong and important." What motivated him was: "Jesus is victor!" and everything else faded away. This hope and faith shaped all his relationships with people for the rest of his life. He had reached a higher plane. The former plane of the struggle and involvement with unclean demonic spirits was justifiable, since it was forced upon him – any honest person who knew this man could see that. But it was not and is not justifiable to revert back to that plane. At a certain point what mattered and what truly happened is that the Lord Jesus was victorious – and in him God the Father through the Holy Spirit. Through a man assigned to the job, the unclean demonic spirit was opposed, overpowered in the name of Jesus, and cast out.

But now what matters and what truly has to happen is that we don't get stuck there. Rather, on the basis of what has been achieved – "Jesus is victor!" – we must move on to the job that lies in front of us. The husk that can encase people, the husk of demonic darkness, is broken. The kernel is free! Why should we be interested in the husk of the shell? Now we have to go to work on the kernel, for the kernel is man in his own flesh. The struggle against the excesses within our flesh is more important than the struggle against Satan. For if Satan is overpowered but we are not willing to overcome ourselves, then sooner or later the husk will form again, and heathen demonic beings will cloud our spirits anew and pull us back into superstition and idolatry (cf. Matt. 12:43–35; Luke 11:24–26).

---

6 This refers to an episode in the Labors of Hercules. See Philip Matyszak, *The Greek and Roman Myths: A Guide to the Classical Stories* (London: Thames & Hudson, 2010).

At first my father had to deal with the demons themselves, but the situation soon changed entirely. He was confronted with people whose inner being had been scarred by demons. They were a bigger obstacle to God than the demons. At first my father had to tackle the dark spirits that shrouded people in order to free them. Later on he had to tackle the *people* themselves – and this is especially true for us today too. Then the dark shroud falls off by itself. For if a person comes into the light and salvation of God, then who is there to be afraid of? Nothing, whether visible or invisible, whether past or present (cf. Rom. 8:38) can have any power over those who belong to the Savior because they have experienced his victory over their own flesh and have made room [in their lives] for God's truth and his righteousness in Christ Jesus.

6

The Ongoing Battle

MY FATHER'S MINISTRY WAS CONFIRMED by the way his congregation blossomed with a new spirit, and he was given a breather. But this breather was not a time to relax. Life swirled around him like a swift river, which was obvious by the constant flow of visitors, who came uninvited. Thousands of people confidently flocked to Möttlingen, bringing their inner or physical needs, and my father did not have to look for work.[1] He had become a spiritual counselor with the full authority of God's spirit. He did not need to go looking for people. They came to *him* and listened to his advice. It was no wonder that in spite of all the taxing work, a feeling of Sabbath rest was felt by anyone who joined the ministry of this man out of love for the kingdom of God. It was also no wonder that others were upset because there was no pattern, no human guidelines, that could be learned and copied. My father's life and work varied from day to day according to the different needs, but always in *one* spirit that rolled on like a stream. His life was a *battle* until he died – that was the determining element in all his activity as a spiritual counselor and fatherly friend to many people.

This battle had flared up in an innocent person, yet someone on whom Satan had been given permission to wield his power, like on Job (1:6–12, 2:1–6).[2] The battle, once ignited, evolved into a ministry, under God's guidance, that never ceased.

---

1 See Zündel, 158–204.

2 The father Blumhardt saw the similarity between Job's experience and what happened to Gottliebin Dittus in that they both were not caused by human sin. In both cases the events were sovereignly permitted by God to bring him glory.

Oppressive Powers Fight Back

WHAT MY FATHER ACCOMPLISHED in the first conflict equipped him for his interactions with everyone he met. A concealed inner wrestling with some invisible power would quietly relax – the tension would ease – in a person when they brought their burdens to him. These invisible powers bound and affected people in many different ways. The people themselves were unaware of them, but these powers would confront the spiritual counselor. It was not intelligence or experience, Bible knowledge or other human reasoning or therapy that brought the help which radiated from my father. It was the warrior fighting against the invisible spirits that were binding people. The struggle which engrossed this pastor and counselor in the beginning for a single person and forced him into battle with the slogan "Jesus is victor!" took place later on without any particular action for many people, yes, for everyone who came near him.

When a commander in chief has slain the enemy's general, he then has to deal merely with the enslaved forces of the enemy, in order to bring deliverance to individuals. That is what it was like for my father after his first victory. All his successes were fruits of that first victory and further victories. This is why many mentally or emotionally disturbed people felt an urge to come close to him. But also people with certain physical ailments (ailments that stemmed from emotional bondages) confided their needs to my father with amazing trust. These people hoped for help from God, who rules from the visible world to the invisible world. Anyone who didn't understand this supposed that he was a quack doctor with hidden remedies. But the man could in no way be accused, for he had authority from God. This authority was the only basis for the founding of the asylum at Bad Boll. The best name I can think of for Bad Boll is "The Battlefield."

No Time to Rest

IN SHORT, MY FATHER was given a breather, but there was no time to rest. There were plenty of battles, and as more people came, new types of emotional bondage came to light. Some of these took a heavy toll on him, in terms of both inner anguish and physical strain. It was a matter of holding on to the light he had received, a light that could shine into all powers of darkness. But the worldly powers surrounding my father tried to extinguish the light. Most people were not aware of how hard he and his helpers had to wrestle for this light, so that it would not be extinguished by the pressures of normal daily life as time went on. Of course no one talked about this anymore. The events at Möttlingen had become public and could no longer be concealed. But what continued to take place could be kept secret, simply because there are no words to properly describe such internal battles. That is why any publication of these inner battles is more likely to be a hindrance than a help. For those who wanted to see, it was enough to know that such hidden, inner struggle is completely justified and should be fought by authorized warriors. We can see the results in the testimonies to God's grace bestowed on people according to *God's* will. These results should not be seen as my father's work; they should come to light as works of God and they should turn people to rejoice in the Lord – not in my father.

From this time on my father, the spiritual counselor, became known in public as a man of intercession. His prayers were linked to the struggles he had fought, and it was his prayers that people who experienced something noticed most.[3] But today we have to say that my father's prayer (which did bring results) was not the same as what we usually think of when we pray for people today. The power of Christ, the victor, freely performed miracles according to God's will without any specific intercession. In no way can we speak of Bad Boll as a faith-healing institution. Those appeared only later on and at other places. My father couldn't stand the idea of prayer being demoted to a medicine. He simply couldn't understand how people could pray and pray for someone as though God could be forced by intense prayer to do something he actually did not want to do. That's why he warned against urgent, demanding prayer about human concerns and held strictly to Jesus' words: "Seek first the kingdom of God . . . then all the rest will fall into place" (Matt. 6:33), and also, "Your father knows what you need before you ask him" (Matt. 6:8). Instead of just interceding, my father went to battle – he went to the front line for others. But if people were not willing to fight too, or if they were not able to sacrifice themselves for the kingdom of God (in whatever shape or form that might take in their lives), then every petition was in vain.

Surely nobody believes that one person's prayer for another person will work mechanically, like medicine in a doctor's hand. True, the forceful presence of a person can have an effect, but this is something different, and will sooner or later completely fall back into the flesh, like all psychologically induced miracle cures, which are forced by human coercion. Therefore the Savior also warns us to beware of those who perform miracles in his name

---

3 See Zündel, 476–486. This is conveyed in a lively way by the elder Blumhardt's pastoral writings in *Ausgewählte Schriften*, vol. III: *Seelsorge* (Metz: Franz u. Sternberg, 1996), 3–34.

(Matt. 7:22–23), if they do not understand the will of the Father in heaven and put it first – if they simply intercede for people and their wants and their desire to get better.

God Supplies the Strength

AS LONG AS HE LIVED, my father continued to do battle. Sometimes, in the hustle and bustle of daily life, the battle seemed to flag and the light required for it seemed to die out. It was at such a time that I was given the chance to support my father, though I had not asked for it.[4] In those days I got an insight into how his soul anguished over the mighty powers of Satan still raging in the world. Too many people wanted to take advantage of this man's gifts for themselves, which meant they were like people throwing wet straw and leaves on a few glowing embers. I realized that, as time went on, my father himself made the mistake of feeling too sorry for people – he worried for them so much that it wasn't a help for God's kingdom.

In this connection I have to say that this mistake continued to be a problem. Later on we too – along with our zeal for God and his kingdom – wanted to arrange everything more or less to please people. Whenever we make this mistake, we get overburdened. Sure, we are still serving God, but it can get so bad that only a minimal amount of time is left over for what is of value to God, while by far the greater amount of time and strength is used to meet the needs and wishes of people. Take this as a rule of thumb: God never overburdens his servants. If we are overburdened, it is because people are putting burdens on us. We are accepting burdens that other people load onto us, even if it looks like we are serving God alone. It simply is our wretched flesh that butts in everywhere and in the end claims for itself our church services and all God's gifts of grace in Christ Jesus. These gifts were meant to be used to further righteousness and truth without regard to any person. In the end God is downgraded to be but a servant for men and women, and Christ, too, in many cases, becomes merely the Savior for our own needs.

This explains my position today, in contrast to the position my father had. When I recognized the mistake of getting overburdened, it was almost too late – I was overtaxed almost to the point of death.[5] Then I considered

---

4 Compare Werner Jäckh, *Blumhardt, Vater und Sohn und ihre Welt* (Stuttgart: Steinkopf, 1977), 103f; 119f.

5 Christoph Blumhardt went through some painful experiences. After losing several of his closest coworkers, his wife became seriously ill in the spring of 1889. Then, at the beginning of April, Blumhardt himself became so ill that he had to withdraw for six months into seclusion in the newly built house at Eckwälden. From that time on, Blumhardt reduced his public activities

where the mistake lay, certain that *God* would not have overburdened me. I found out, for instance, that the excessive amount of preaching that I was doing was of no value to God. I was doing it just because people enjoyed it so much, but their delight in listening to me did not help them to put the Word of God into practice, as I hoped it would. So I stopped preaching so much. We were also doing other things just because it made certain people feel more at home. But once God himself had given us a fright, we could no longer spend time pleasing people.

The Inner Battle Remains

THIS EXPLAINS MANY THINGS which people have noticed where my position is different from my father's. It also explains why at that time the battle was less free and less pure and almost died out. But it was not to die. God shook his servant awake again through certain events and thrust him into new battles. In those days I stood at my father's side and privately experienced with him a lot of hidden opposition to the kingdom of God but also a lot of deliverance. Outwardly it was a time when people swarmed to Bad Boll, but inwardly we were faced with untold dilemmas, difficulties, and deep troubles, which occupied us day and night. If God's special strength had not sustained us, we would have physically succumbed.

During this time the mistake mentioned above created other problems. Because we spent too much time and strength serving people, our workload doubled. And because we did not dare to cut back on what we were doing for people, it was obvious that we would not be able to continue like this very long. So a great longing seized us for the struggle to be over and often prompted us to zealously tackle all sorts of human bondages. As a result we sometimes went our own way. We have to admit today that we sometimes tried to force something when it was not God's time for it. So wrong things crept in, which of course took their toll. For in godly matters everything is avenged, especially anything bordering on disobedience. God is a zealous God toward his servants; he is called an avenger. We say this in praise of God's faithfulness, for without his righteousness we would have perished. However, throughout everything, the light of Jesus Christ continued to shine and there was plenty to encourage us, so that even though we were deeply broken in spirit, we could still look forward with full confidence to the end of the struggle. We just had to learn more and more that not we but Jesus Christ will win the victory.

---

greatly. Christoph Blumhardt, *Ansprachen, Predigten, Reden, Briefe 1865–1917*, 190f; also notes 56 and 57.

In this connection, my father himself experienced an inner conclusion to the struggle. Shortly before he departed from this world, he had a vision of the Lord he had been called to serve, and this was a turning point. He experienced something similar to Moses. When Moses arrived at the Promised Land – the goal of his pilgrimage – he was permitted to see it from Mount Nebo but he could not enter it with his people (Deut. 34:1–4). Similarly, my father was shown in his spirit the imminent renewal of creation, the renewal he had spent so many years fighting for and still hoped to experience. In this vision, he heard these words as if God were speaking to him: "Eternal peace shall yet come on earth. The curses on earth shall be turned into blessings. Zion will appear, and you will sing with them."[6] From that day on my father got ready for something special. He put everything in order, knowing he was at a turning point. Since he was not sure what would happen to him, or what would take place, he deliberately placed himself into God's hands. Very soon a severe illness came over him, consuming his body. He died on February 25, 1880.[7]

Until he died my father carried in his spirit the comfort given to him personally about the coming of the kingdom of God. But his death was difficult both for him and for us. We were well aware that the struggle was not over yet and that he had not lived to experience the goal as he had hoped. We were guilty for those dark days because we had been overzealous. But a new light dawned for us through the painful but healing judgment of the Holy Spirit. We became aware at least partially of mistakes we had not noticed before, and the Lord led us – those whom he chastised – back onto new paths of grace. We could continue the struggle with new light and new hope. "Jesus is victor!" was still the call, now even more so and for us too.

Fighting against the Flesh

AS WE FOUGHT AGAINST many different satanic powers and longed to be freed at last, the other part of the struggle slowly came to the fore: the fight against the flesh. At first this fight was unclear, because many afflictions still caused us to wrestle against principalities and powers. I will refrain from further discussion of this experience. At the time we also did not ponder over it or try to understand everything. In fact, we did not have the right to give it too much thought. And so it is also not necessary or possible to describe these hidden experiences by telling about the different events. In short, the time came when the battle against darkness that we had been

6 See Zündel, 512–519.
7 See Zündel, 520–524.

assigned to fight since the days of Möttlingen came to an end. In times past the ups and downs of life had often affected us painfully. Not only had my father died, but so had all the older coworkers,[8] and we felt lonely. But, standing on a solid foundation, we were on fire that Jesus, the Lord, would lead us by his strong hand in all things, just as he had done in the past. He would lead his cause to victory for us, as well as for the whole world. Inwardly we put ourselves fully at God's disposal, ready for whatever the future would bring.

We did not have to wait long. God showed us very clearly *that* our attitude had to change and *how*, now that the battle begun at Möttlingen had come to an end, as he wanted it to. A new light broke through. All of us who belonged to the inner circle felt the will of God with such power that we, newly united, did not hesitate for a moment to turn to the new path. We could see the new path through the following clear recognition that God was giving to us: the battle against Satan may end, but we human beings with our selfish nature in the flesh continue to oppose God. Just as when something indescribably great and holy draws near, a great fear seized us, and we wondered how we would stand in the face of what was coming. As if out of the sanctuary of God it came to us: "You can stand your ground against Satan in my name, and against hell, and you can also stand in the face of death in my name, but before me you cannot stand, unless I live within you totally."

Now more than ever we recognized what a huge hindrance the flesh is, and now it was important to really take on the battle against our own flesh and blood. We did not resist, and so our change in attitude was soon noticed by others. Many people did not understand, but our path had been shown to us unequivocally by God; hence our battle took on a new dimension. It became a battle to which we now could challenge our friends by telling them: "Die, so that Jesus may live!"

In those days we were in difficult circumstances for a longer period of time in regards to our personal lives.[9] In our inner being we sensed death, even if nobody noticed anything outwardly. But God gave us the grace at least to begin fixing our thoughts and hearts solely on surrendering our "self" into the death of Christ, so that Jesus might live and so that we

---

8 Gottliebin Dittus, January 26, 1872; his mother, Doris (Johanna Dorothea) Blumhardt, July 6, 1886; Johann Georg "Hansjörg" Dittus, March 20, 1888; Friedrich Zündel, June 9, 1891.

9 This refers to the illnesses occurring in 1889. Mentioned in detail by E. Jäckh, *Christoph Blumhardt, Ein Zeuge des Reiches Gottes* (Stuttgart: Evang. Missionsverl., 1950), 121ff.; and in Christoph Blumhardt, *Eine Auswahl*, vol. 2, 585ff., a reprint of a circular letter from Christoph Blumhardt to his friends from July 1889. See also the *Vertrauliche Blätter* for this year.

would not exist merely to live for ourselves. That Jesus alone has the right to prevail and that we can stand only *in* him became even clearer to us through a serious ordeal. Suddenly we were confronted with the near death of a family member.[10] In this incident (which many people heard about) we experienced a miraculous healing, and we saw this as a seal that Jesus Christ would not reject us. In quietness we were to continue fighting for the kingdom of God – fighting no longer against the powers of darkness but against ourselves, so that Jesus could reign over us and within us, just as he reigns over all powers and principalities and authorities in heaven and on earth and under the earth.

Where We Stand Today

WE OWE OUR READERS these historical notes about our life from Möttlingen to the present so that they can judge [for themselves] our position today. We are well aware that what is described here could easily be misinterpreted. But we have to appeal to a more spiritual side of history. Anyone can shout at us: You are deceived! In fact, even more so recently, because heavy judgments have come over our family and it might look as though our cause has come to nothing.[11] All I can say is that this was only right and fair, part of the justice promised to us, which we had to accept from God as part of his new regime. It took judgments to make us clearly aware of this. Much of the nature of the flesh which penetrates us simply cannot be eradicated in any other way. In all of this we realize what these judgments mean for us, and we will not resist them but praise God, even if those who received these manifestations of God may fall right and left or have to change their lives entirely. We should not be confused by this, but rather be more convinced that what we have come to know to be true will also become a reality in our lives. God wants to establish himself, even if it is at the expense of our lives. Yet it is not about us at all, or our story, it is all

---

10 Blumhardt's wife, Emilie, nee Bräuninger, faced a serious illness after the birth of their daughter Gottliebin on January 3, 1889. See the reports in the *Vertrauliche Blätter*, February 1889 and March 1889. Blumhardt reports about his own illness in April 1889.

11 In the first edition, that published in the *Vertrauliche Blätter*, Christoph Blumhardt adds to this chapter a section called "News" in which he tells about the events he is referring to: the sudden death of the head gardener, Johannes Ehrath in July 1894 (not 1895, as Blumhardt writes there), the emigration of his brother Nathanael to New Zealand on February 2, 1895, and also the separation from his brother-in-law Emil Brodersen, who had been the manager of the estate. See also E. Jäckh, *Christoph Blumhardt*, 129–131. In July 1894 was the bad accident at the well, where three men of Bad Boll suffered death, as well as the severe accusations against Christoph Blumhardt by Friedrich Bodelschwingh. See Christoph Blumhardt, *Ansprachen, Predigten, Reden, Briefe 1865–1917*, vol. 2, 41, 42, 44–45.

about the battle for the truth of God's kingdom. Today, all who love Jesus Christ and in his name are waiting for the kingdom of God are involved in this battle. Judge for yourselves whether we are right when we say: "Die, then Jesus will live!"

The battle of our Lord and Master Jesus Christ ended in his death, because it was through his resurrection from the dead that God could reveal his glory. In the end, his church also cannot be victorious in any other way than by all members surrendering their own self, their flesh, totally to their Lord and Master, in his blood. The church has to let the life of Jesus Christ, the resurrected one, come to its own in the church and be fully revealed on earth. It is more important for Jesus to be victor in this battle than in any other battle. Even if everything has been achieved – Satan defeated, forgiveness of sin made possible, yes, even the possibility given to enter into glory after death – all this is put into question again if the flesh is not conquered, if humanity itself, as it lives and moves on earth, does not submit to God's claim. Only then can there be peace on earth, only then can we rest in God's Sabbath, which will come anew to all creation. Let us keep focused on this highest goal and not get weary. Every individual is called to help fight in this battle, and every individual may joyfully cry out at any time in this battle: "Jesus is victor! Jesus lives!"

PART III

The Spirit's Work

Movement and Resistance

7

Only a Small Beginning

IN ORDER TO SAY MORE about our present attitude, we need to turn our thoughts to what my father experienced next at Möttlingen. I have tried to explain how I feel today about the "struggle," as my father called it. What followed the struggle he called "the revival" [or "the awakening"] in his congregation. Pastor Zündel, in his biography of my father, calls this section, "The Movement of Repentance."[1] It was at the end of the year 1843, Christmas time, when the whole situation in which my father found himself suddenly changed. "Look, I am coming soon!" (Rev. 3:11, 22:7, 22:12, 22:20). This word of the Savior came true for this warrior who was often taxed to the point of exhaustion, since he could see no end in sight and his relationship with the outside world was getting more and more difficult. How often had he been told: "You will end up being ridiculed and in disgrace, just like everyone else who gets involved with demons." My father knew he had not entered into this struggle out of curiosity or foolish religious zeal. He knew he had been compelled to follow obediently in spite of his own reluctance. If he had not had a clear conscience regarding this, then very likely those voices within him would have won, which whispered: "Just drop everything and get out of this whole affair as best you can." For, as I have just said, he simply could see no end to this strenuous conflict.

But then came the call: "I am coming soon. Jesus is victor!" These words were first spoken by someone beaten down in deep affliction, when the intense struggle with powers of darkness culminated.[2] Like a cleansing stream, these words penetrated into the spiritual life of the Möttlingen

---

1 Zündel, 158–204.
2 Zündel, 150–151.

congregation and created an awakening – first in individuals and then in everyone who belonged to the congregation. Choking in the morass of sin and superstition (superstition that killed all true life), one after another people raised their heads out of the mire and realized with horror how wrong their lives had been. "Only Jesus the Lord – the judge – can help and heal!" This was now the single prevailing thought. No one hesitated long – without any reservations they confessed their own guilt, their part in the corruption of the whole community. They did not rest until they had received through a specific word of grace the cleansing they were aching for. This cleansing was confirmed through signs of physical healing by the life-giving spirit of Christ. The following song of praise was relived a hundred times over: "Praise the Lord, my soul; all my inmost being, praise his holy name. Praise the Lord, my soul . . . the Lord, who forgives all your sins and heals all your diseases" (Ps. 103:1–3).

The Awakening of the Spirit

THIS AWAKENING OF THE SPIRIT of Christ in sinners and sick people alike was a foundation stone for my father. It continued to give him strength to use new ways to work for God's kingdom. The awakening of the congregation was a continuation of the struggle that had been fought there. Spirits of unbelief and superstition form the background for the superstitious on earth. When Christ's spirit entered among these spirits, the awakening was a reflection in living people who had become aware of the Spirit's entry. This enabled Christ to work in their physical lives to his honor. That is why this awakening was also a *struggle*. It was an inner fight within those who were awakened, who now had to be warriors against anything ungodly. Outwardly the struggle also challenged all previous customs and habits of professing Christians. The nature of this awakening seemed strange to other believers. Something about the awakening of the congregation at Möttlingen was like a judgment, knocking at the doors of believers who had been living in peace and contentment, taking pride in their faith. This explains the rather bittersweet affirmation of my father's friends, who again were afraid that he was starting something new. Only a few of his friends took part in the experience wholeheartedly and joyfully. Even though hundreds of people came from afar to Möttlingen and sensed the spirit of truth that ruled there, and even though my father himself was officially recognized, still he remained isolated in this second experience. The result could quite easily have been the formation of a sect, also because my father was strongly advised by some people to disassociate himself from the [state] church, which had taken measures to confine and dampen the movement.[3]

My father frequently found himself in very awkward positions. In the end he was even forbidden to welcome members of other congregations into his house.[4] The fact that he did not form a sect is proof enough for us today that it was the spirit of Christ – who wants to reach everyone – that brought about the awakening in Möttlingen. In no way was it the result of my father's human charisma. The inner battle brought about the awakening, and to this day the hallmark of our attitude to life is engaging in this fight. We also cannot help it if, as our life progresses toward God and his kingdom, it takes shape in ways that seem strange to other believers. Then as now when we experience such an awakening in people it usually happens quietly, yes, even in a certain seclusion.

The lovely uplifting power that emanated from my father's experiences penetrated far and wide like a sweet fragrance and attracted thousands, but it could be fully understood only by those who were involved. Nevertheless, in these circles the sun shone for a long time and could not be darkened. The sun had broken through the dark clouds, and it blessed with its warmth everyone who exposed themselves to its rays, causing them to grow and flourish with new life. In previously darkened hearts God's grace broke forth, bringing light everywhere and apparently changing everything down to the very bottom. Everything in the past, all trouble and temptation, every battle and all ridicule regarding the struggle, all muck and filth was forgotten in the face of the fresh new life germinating in the rejuvenated congregation, which was living and breathing in the strength of God. The aroma of death had changed into the aroma of life (2 Cor. 2:15–16), for even people's physical health was awakened to new life.

Squandering God's Grace

WITHOUT ANY EFFORT, the Word had an effect on real life. Without much talk things changed – a word spoken became the first step for God to act.[5] Works of the heavenly Father became visible in such a convincing,

---

3 We can see how strongly the elder Blumhardt resisted the idea of separation from the Lutheran state church by his attitude already during the time he was a vicar in Iptingen; see Zündel, 50–54. Later on he also resisted the thought of separation; see for example Zündel, 339–340.

4 See Zündel, 219–225, about this affair (which actually took place in 1846, not 1844). A portion of the authority's edict is reprinted in Johann Christoph Blumhardt, *Der Kampf in Möttlingen*, I, 1, 355ff. and explained in I, 2, 161ff.

5 In the Bible, God's spoken word and his actions coincide. See Ps. 33:9. When God "speaks" it

natural way that even the word "miracle" died on our lips. These were such a natural part of life that they could be picked up on the streets, so to speak. But, of course, this was also detrimental to the ministry, because among the thousands upon thousands of people who visited Möttlingen, many were merely curious or looking only for physical help. The future shone in a bright light. It shone with the great hope of the apostles. You could feel the salvation of God, and it was a delight to behold beginnings that showed how easily God's accomplishments could be attained. This sun of grace and truth, which had emerged solely in the name of Jesus, remained the most telling witness in my father's life. It was a constant source of encouragement for him. For many who were close to him, to experience heavenly things meant that they were actually able to see eternal treasures and to know that they would be able to see them again and again. We also were allowed to live in the rays of this sun for decades. For the rays of this sun broke through again and again, reviving us, witnessing to us, and calling us – the children of that time – into battles for God's kingdom and into experiences within God's kingdom.

Yet just because of this fighting and these continuing experiences, first my father and then we could not remain at the stage of merely marveling at those refreshing times with the Savior. Rather, in the midst of these happy times of revival in his congregation, my father met at every step something unconquered and human, which caused him inner fear and concern. Without really understanding what was wrong, he was in a way schooled by God through his battles, so that he knew he could not reckon that through such a conversion of the whole congregation something completed and secure was won for the kingdom of God. Instead he was overcome with fear and trembling, and it was obvious to him that if nothing further would happen with the people, then this movement would pass, and the whole experience would remain but an isolated bizarre phenomenon, without any essential gain for the kingdom of God on earth.

Even so, something from eternity truly broke in, bringing great thoughts and concrete signs of the promises that are given in the scriptures regarding the kingdom of God. The spirit of the prophets came alive; Isaiah, with his hope for Zion was practically present; a hope for the salvation of all nations emerged, which was fully scriptural and which put the emphasis on personal salvation in the background. An international society gathered in the

---

"comes to pass," because God's word carries within it the power to act. See Christoph Friedrich Blumhardt, *Eine Auswahl*, vol. 2, 576ff.

parsonage at Möttlingen and later on at Bad Boll. Still, my father could not shake off his anxiety and finally cried out to God: "If the Spirit from on high is not poured out anew, even this amount of grace and truth is not worth much." In fact, its worth was even offset because the grace and truth given at Möttlingen tended to be in opposition to traditional Christian forms. Since the Möttlingen movement could not be incorporated into the church or any sect, it was in a much more dangerous position within Christianity and was therefore all the more likely to be forgotten. No traditional church or sect could embrace it with a hearty welcome, because from the very beginning it countered certain church ordinances and traditions, and this annoyed churchgoers of all confessions.

The Greater End

SOMETHING WAS STILL MISSING. My father was well aware that the movement at Möttlingen as it was – and as it was viewed from the outside – was in great danger of petering out. This is why he never invited people to join Möttlingen or Bad Boll. Instead, he pointed beyond that, as if to say: "All this is only a small beginning and you must not get stuck here." We had received something like a divine shove, through which we were propelled into this movement, in order to be driven on toward a far greater goal. That person is foolish who feels this shove but instead of being propelled forward, turns around to admire the thrust. Has not this been the mistake from time immemorial? After receiving a measure of grace, instead of looking ahead in order to attain the final goal, people turn around to admire the grace they have received, and in the end they make an idol of it. In this way the apostles and prophets can also be made into idols. And similarly, people have admired the Reformation of the sixteenth century more as a reformation than as a thrust forward.

To do this is the same as getting stuck; and getting stuck, standing still, or marveling at the gift or grace one has received was something my father just could not do. But he did not know what to do in order to move forward. In this predicament he at least made the right move, by turning to God and by submitting both himself and his congregation to judgment. He grasped the rope of hope – hope in the *working* of the spirit of God that can cause heights and depths to shudder and quake, and that is even able to transform the whole human race (which the mere "Christian" spirit is not able to do). In this hope my father found his only staff[6] that did not break.

---

6 Christoph Blumhardt uses the word "staff" to describe something that people can hold on to, something that gives them hope. See chapter 13, in which Blumhardt describes three false staffs.

This hope was his salvation, without which he would have perished, and without which we also would not be able to endure.

One thing he did not fully recognize, which we had to realize in later years after hoping and waiting for a long time: namely, that such an outpouring of the Holy Spirit can occur only when certain conditions are met by us human beings. He did not fully recognize that the battle against darkness is not the final battle. When all is said and done, the invisible powers of darkness cannot prevent God from working in the visible world; they cannot prevent him from doing what has to be done for people. But a human being, who lives on earth and has a spirit originally breathed into him by God, can by nursing his own ego plant himself in God's way so firmly that God is indeed hindered from giving him the Spirit. And yet God wants to give us the Spirit because he does not want to let us perish in the flesh. In the end what counts is the battle in the visible world against the flesh, against a certain selfishness in humankind. People would love to make God himself be their servant, just so they could sneak into heaven to get to the blessedness they so desire.

Today we confess openly: my father's hope [for a new outpouring of the Holy Spirit] cannot be fulfilled simply by praying, "Give us the Holy Spirit!" Granted, the Savior said: "Ask for the Holy Spirit!" and "If you then, who are evil, know how to give good gifts to your children, how much more will your Father in heaven give the Holy Spirit to those who ask him!" (Luke 11:13). But he of course presupposed that those who ask are not people who are secretly pampering their own flesh or who desire the spirit of God merely to feather their own nest. The Savior and the apostles take it for granted that the people who pray have taken up the battle against themselves and have won the victory. They assume these people have died with Christ and risen with Christ into a completely new life. It is to such people that the promise is given: "You will receive whatever you ask for in prayer" (Matt. 21:22; John 14:13, 15:16, 16:23). The greater the gift for which we approach God, the deeper the judgment has to penetrate into our flesh, so that our flesh has died before the divine gift is given. God cannot lay his gifts into a dirty bowl, a dish that welcomes all manner of iniquity and evil. The vessel has to be holy into which a holy gift is to be placed. A person has to be freed from their own egoism, in which they want to serve themselves. They have to be totally on fire for God, or they will pray in vain for the Holy Spirit. In the same way, spiritual movements like that in Möttlingen can run very deep and still in the end disappear into the sand. Yes, such spiritual movements are actually even harmful at the end of the day if they do not lead to further results: namely, to real testimonies to God, which give glory to God and not to people, and through which Jesus himself lives and reigns.

Misunderstandings and Corrections

IN THIS REGARD it is wrong to say, as many people have often said: "The Spirit of God has already been poured out. In fact it must have been poured out to make such a dying with Jesus possible." Anyone who says this has underestimated the height and depth [of the power] of the Holy Spirit, which grants times of revelation[7] and prepares for the last revelation of Jesus Christ by making changes on earth in people who are covenanted with God. These changes are prerequisites for a new heaven and a new earth. The history of God's kingdom as it is laid out for us in the Holy Bible gives adequate evidence that when God starts his work in men and women it entails a certain dying to their own flesh, and this dying process has to reach a certain completion before promises are fulfilled.

Abraham had to surrender everything he called his own, even his only son (Gen. 22:1–19), before the promise was confirmed and sworn to by an oath. Moses' selfishness, as well as that of the people around him, had to be broken through God's leading before the glory of the Lord – the revelation of the great God and Savior of humankind – could ensure the victory over Egypt and before the basic guidelines for life could be presented in the Law. And unless those guidelines were obeyed, no further promises could be fulfilled. Almost no one fully realizes this, even though in biblical history we see that, despite all the promises given to the people of Israel as a nation, it never attained the promises given to it (Heb. 11:1–39). The only people who welcomed the promised Messiah were those who listened to the voice of one calling in the wilderness (Isa. 40:3; John 1:23) and then surrendered themselves even more fully to the voice of Jesus himself, whose words meant dying to the flesh. This maxim: "Anyone who loves their life, will lose it" (John 12:25; Matt. 10:39, 16:25; Luke 17:33) is and always was a fundamental principle in God's history regardless of all promises. The apostles had to be dead to self for the outpouring of the Holy Spirit to occur. It may well be that many others who had not fully died to themselves took part in that grace given to the apostles, but this happened in the presupposition that they would make good, as it were, on what they missed during the Savior's lifetime. They knew they were in danger of losing the Holy Spirit again if they did not die to themselves. The Judaizing Christians did gradually

---

7 See Johann Christoph Blumhardt, *Ausgewählte Schriften*, vol. 1, *Schriftauslegung* (Metz: Franz u. Sternberg, 1996), 117ff.; 139ff.; 317ff.

lose the Spirit that could actively reveal God's truth because they thought they had to keep the Jewish traditions (which represented the flesh). That is why the Holy Spirit, the spirit of revelation and renewed life, had to retreat, even though a certain "Christian" spirit – born of revelations to the early Christians – was painstakingly kept alive. This "Christian" spirit was kept alive only by using worldly means – that is, powers of the state and money – which have played a greater role in Christianizing the nations than the spirit of revelation. The Holy Spirit, which can reveal God's will, flees whenever any form of human selfishness is nurtured or clung to. May God protect us from making the same mistake as those who think they merely have to remind God of his promises in order for them to be fulfilled!

The Significance of Spiritual Movements

HAVING SAID THE ABOVE, this does not mean that we should look down in any way on a movement or a collective urge by many people at once to seek for the kingdom of God. There are plenty of people who think that such ringing of the alarm bell only disrupts their normal church life. They mistakenly think it is good enough if word and sacrament are kept on an even keel from one decade to the next. They think they just have to make sure that in their encounters with unbelievers, nothing disturbs what they believe must be right because it is the confession of the church into which they were born – this confession has to be preserved from century to century. Not a mouse should stir, not a puff of wind should blow – everybody should just sit pretty, submit to the church organization, and partake of the means of grace.

Mark you, I am well aware how many fanatical uprisings occur in a desire for new life that are merely the result of human efforts. Certainly these create more harm than good. I also do not want to minimize in any way traditional doctrines and rules which during low times were guidelines for the way of salvation throughout the centuries. Such regulations are often and in certain conditions comparable to the shell which encases the kernel in a nut. The kernel is able to sprout and bring forth fruit. The shell protects the kernel while it is in storage. But we know that such a kernel, enclosed in its shell, is destined to be placed into the soil, where it will burst its shell and start to develop. Imagine now that for centuries Christianity has carried this living kernel in the name of Jesus. This kernel is the Son of God: Jesus, who walked on earth in the flesh, passing on the thoughts of God to his contemporaries through signs and wonders; Jesus, who preached about the kingdom of God, saying that it was already breaking in and is coming in order to bring God's salvation to all the world; Jesus, who died as a substitute for all humankind in order to slay their own flesh and carnal thoughts; Jesus, who rose from the dead as the first born in order to say: "Because I live, you also will live" (John 14:19); Jesus, who sits at the right hand of God in order to govern and be victorious until every knee has bowed to his name (1 Cor. 15:24–28; Phil. 2:10ff.) under the one true will of the Creator of life; Jesus, who will come again to carry out the last of God's [mighty] deeds when he will judge humankind and the whole of creation and lift them out of the woes of sin and death. If then Christianity has safely stored this kernel for centuries in the shell of church regulations, even until our time, this certainly does not mean that this kernel has to stay in its shell forever and be adored as a mystery. Obviously at its appointed time the kernel will sprout, and as a prerequisite it has to first be planted into creation so that all created things may find their true divine existence again through this life in Jesus.

If this is so, we should not be surprised if from time to time the kernel within the shell shows some movement. After all, it has life and wants to break through the shell. This is the natural urge of Jesus living within people who seek for the kingdom of God. Sometimes, if exploited by people in an untimely manner by self-will, this desire can lead to deformed lifestyles that squander the energies of life. But sometimes God himself stimulates growth or movement so that the vitality within the kernel is kept alive. Therefore, popular or mass movements in the direction of God's kingdom can be either true or false – stimulated by God or merely generated by human beings. I consider the Reformation to be stimulated by God, as well as other later movements that grew from that same ground and gave a new direction to Christian life. In all humility, I would also include the events at Möttlingen. Even though these events affected smaller circles, and even though many people view them as insignificant in the complex whole of Christianity, we have reason enough to see in these events the spirit of Christ, the spirit of grace and revelation.

Habits imprison people. So it simply is a fact that the conflicting interests behind our habits have to be confronted and challenged again and again. Whenever we recognize something as false, we have to abolish it. And whenever we do that, many people will gather around the attempt.

Recognizing God's History

WE MUST NOT OVERLOOK a certain great danger for the kingdom of God – namely, that those who are moved when God initiates a movement tend to give more importance to the movement than to the Spirit that caused the movement. Popular mass movements can blind us; false forms can develop rapidly and claim our respect solely because they are new. When you plant a nut, it is the kernel that determines the fruit. Even so for religious movements: the kernel is decisive, not the movement, if it is to bear fruit for God's kingdom. [The leaders of] any popular mass movement for the kingdom of God should be wary of any growth that does not come from the spirit of Christ. They should guard against giving space to any life that is not the life of Jesus Christ. Otherwise the door will soon be wide open again for selfish dealings, and our carnal desires will merely get sprinkled with holy water.

This is how you can tell whether a movement is truly seeking for God's kingdom: it does not try to get bigger and bigger; it does not strive to obtain a leading position among other religious bodies. It would rather dwindle to nothing for fear of taking in impure elements, because these impure elements can inflict more harm to the kingdom of God from within the community of Christ than they can from outside in the world. To work passionately for converts – to try and gain members for a certain branch of Christianity, even if this branch originally contained basic truths – is not only dangerous for the unity within the community of Christ on earth, but also for the truth contained in that branch of Christianity itself. The fact is: God adds to the church those whom he wants (Acts 2:47). We should not dare to be pushy, to zealously evangelize anyone who comes near us, thinking that whoever is won for us is won for God.

Another way to recognize a movement truly seeking for God's kingdom is when – in spite of the power with which it breaks forth – it retains a quality of gentleness and humility, just like Jesus and his apostles knew how to do. The revolution that the kingdom of God is bringing to all humanity will be orchestrated by God, not people. The movement that John the Baptist set in motion, directed toward God's kingdom, and the movement that surged around Jesus – which was in opposition to the religious views of that time – both contain the same rule of life: "You who are awakened are like sheep among wolves (Matt. 10:16). You have no teeth and no other weapons because God wants to do everything himself. All you have to do is follow the truth."

This rule of life gives us the criteria for judging all movements seeking for God's kingdom that have come into being during the course of history. The movement in itself is not important. What is important is that the principles of God's truth and God's justice that it represents are demonstrated and bring light into the world. We don't need a brief revival of Christian qualities in new forms. We are not looking for entertainment in the monotony of church development. No, the crucial elements in a religious movement are what come from Jesus and the Spirit, gifts that can be given and will last forever. I couldn't care less how the churches in apostolic times arose and developed. What interests me are the life-forces of justice and truth that people found in the name of Jesus and that ruled their lives. These life-forces are eternal and still bring forth fruit for the kingdom of God to this very day. Movements with such life-forces will continue to arise until the last great movement comes that will flood through all nations with the single cry: "The Lord is coming!"

I could also give examples from the history of God's kingdom during Old Testament times in Israel. Through individual people who were fighting for God, movements of repentance were set in motion again and again that brought the light of God to everyone's attention through prophetic words and signs. Think of the story of Samuel. But it would take us off on a tangent to give biblical proof that a movement can be valid even if it threatens to upset church ordinances. Nor do I have time to explain why people are wrong when they condemn on principle any burst of life for God's kingdom in which people also look for new forms and new vessels. I think I have said enough to justify my attitude to the movement at Möttlingen. I also think I am right in saying that the movement at Möttlingen was not prematurely or willfully initiated by human beings, but that it was willed by God. He intended to bring to light again the truth that Jesus lives and has the victory now, just as he was alive and gained the victory at the time of the apostles through the living Word, which worked signs and miracles. It is my firm conviction that Möttlingen should be a lesson for all believers that a life of faith is not a leisurely walk toward blessedness. Instead, we should be eagerly looking forward to these objective realities: to the victory of Jesus Christ and his lordship on earth, to his coming, and to the day when the kingdom of God will be completed.

8

From Victory to Pious Egotism

AT THIS POINT we have to turn our attention away from the divine aspects in this movement and look at the mistakes, which were the result of its human aspects. We have to do this for God's sake, so that no one can say: "If this movement were the work of God, it would have had completely different results." Quite the opposite: we have to recognize that human faults can obstruct the flow of God's truth and God's life. That is what prevented God's next move (to speak in human terms) from following close on the heels of the revival. We have to recognize our mistakes so that we can learn for the future. We have to shoulder our guilt before God and confess it publicly so that anyone who wants to can guard against making the same mistakes.

My father was certainly right to wait [and pray] for the Holy Spirit. Even though the Holy Spirit was obviously already at work, because it brought forth the movement of repentance, still it was needed to a much greater degree in order to create a godly form of life with divine righteousness and real forward movement toward the kingdom of God. But all my father's longings and prayers seemed to have no results. At least he did not experience what he hoped to. So who is to blame? Was he mistaken? No. Rather, we did not know how to respond to this movement in such a way that more grace and more revelation could be poured out by the Holy Spirit. But what was the mistake?

The Willingness to Be Used

MÖTTLINGEN, FOR ALL its fresh wind, still rested on an old foundation – one that was not of permanent value for God's kingdom. It was the foundation of Christian ideas that had developed over the centuries, a theology in which my father was born and raised. Evidently God wanted to see how much could be accomplished with the ways and means the church had become used to and believed in – its dogma and catechism. God used my father as a last attempt, so to speak, to bring people to freedom within the doctrine and forms of worship they were used to. People need to be freed from the curse of their own sinful nature. And then they need to be uplifted to become true members of God's kingdom, members of a true people of God, in whom the living God alone rules in Jesus Christ.

In Möttlingen we saw how the Savior intervened directly, reaching below all the religious ideas that had developed according to church doctrine and traditions. He intervened as the only Shepherd and Overseer of our souls (1 Pet. 2:25). Now it all depended on whether the people who had experienced this grace – who were enjoying the privileges and pleasures of grace – would be willing to let themselves be used as good servants of their Lord. After these people had long lived under the prospect of eternal damnation, they now could see the possibility of salvation, having felt God's abounding grace and love.

Now we had to wait and see whether those who had experienced salvation would be able to give back to God right away what they had received, like money given so that it will bear interest for the Lord (Matt. 25:14–28). Now we would see whether those who were saved would have enough self-denial to look away from themselves and concentrate only on how to be useful servants to their Master, who had given them new tools – life-bringing tools. They ought to be workers in the vineyard, in the vineyard God appoints for each of them. But they were not meant to enjoy the fruit themselves – rather their job was to help bring forth fruit for the Lord (Mark 12:1–12). Sins were to be forgiven; signs should occur; God's kingdom was to come to light in healings of the afflicted and sick, in order that the power of death would be conquered by Jesus Christ, the risen one (Mark 16:17–19). But we are not meant to revel in all these wonderful signs and then rest on our laurels. Instead, these signs should be a source of strength, so that we can continue to work hard, to deny ourselves, and to consider our own interests as rubbish (Phil. 3:8) so that only Christ and the works of God are seen and felt in preparation for the fulfillment of all things.

God may well have hoped this would happen. But we were not yet fit for it. We were a bit like the Prodigal Son (Luke 15:11–24), who found himself longing to fill his stomach with the pods the pigs were eating and then remembered his father's love. But he did not simply comfort himself with his father's love. He also did not come back to his father merely to eat and drink and enjoy the good life again. Instead, when he came home and felt his father's love, he said, "Hire me like one of your servants!" Unfortunately, only a few of those at Möttlingen who had experienced the forgiveness of their sins and the wonderful signs and miracles arrived at this point.

The Poison of Pious Self-Centeredness

INSTEAD, WE FOUND OUT what inner damage the flesh can wreak. The flesh reared its massive head against everything that God wanted to give for his kingdom. Everything we had experienced through Jesus – all of which was a testimony that should have led us forward toward the coming of God's kingdom – called out to us: "Don't use all the grace you have received for yourselves! It is for God, for his purposes, for his goals." But our flesh objected and said: "If something isn't enjoyable for me, I have no use for it." Then the Spirit told us: "Everything has to bear fruit for God, for his truth and his righteousness, otherwise it has no value, even if people are blessed."

Unfortunately, the voice of the flesh has penetrated even into Christianity. Thousands and millions of so-called Christians are so bound by the dictates of their flesh that they see Christ's coming and the hope of his grace only in terms of whether it will make them happy. Not many people [who have been saved] look away from themselves and realize that now their calling is solely to be servants of God, coworkers with God to build his kingdom on earth. Most people think: "I want my sins to be forgiven so I will not be punished. I want a miracle so I can be well again. I want all the grace and revelation of God, I want the celestial circling of heaven with all its heavenly hosts, I want the Son of God to be born in the flesh – just so I can be saved." This self-centeredness was still prevalent in Möttlingen. And by its side was another form of selfishness: members of the established church wanted to use for their own ends whatever was given by God's grace and revelation on their turf. So people tended to assess the movement at Möttlingen from one of these two points of view. Some asked, "How does it benefit the state church?" The others asked, "How does it benefit my personal salvation?" People tried to squeeze the new fellowship into some kind of existing religious box. But the whole character of the newly sprouting life of the Spirit demanded a new form.

Here we face one of the main faults of those people who are called to work in God's kingdom – people who obviously were called, judging by the grace they received from God. The people of Israel already were guilty of this mistake, when they asked, "What will I get out of it if I follow Moses?" They should have been renewed when they felt God's glory and saw the praise of his name on earth. They should have been happy in spite of deprivations and temptations because they knew now for certain that God would take things in hand. Instead they complained stubbornly whenever their physical needs were not met (Exod. 14:10–12, 16:2–3, 17:2–3).

It was the same with the followers of John the Baptist, of the Lord Jesus himself, and of the apostles. What was the problem? The majority of the followers were looking for their own advantages. They did not want to bring forth true fruits of repentance (Matt. 3:8). And when Jesus pointed out that it was a matter of dying to their own lives and working for God and his kingdom – that they had to sacrifice themselves and take up the cross (Matt. 10:37–39; Luke 17:33; John 12:25) – almost everyone left him (John 6:66). Their selfish motives were not going to be met, and only a few could take it: "I'm supposed to torture myself for God's sake? No thanks! That can't be right!"

On what basis did the scribes and Pharisees and Sadducees judge the Lord Jesus? They asked, "How does he benefit our religious order, our ecclesiastical egoism?" For quite a long time they hoped he would become their obedient servant. Then they would have been satisfied with him. But when he did not join their ranks and said, "No one pours new wine into old wineskins" (Mark 2:22), he was doomed, and they sought to kill him (Mark 3:6). This was the fault of the very people whom Jesus longed to gather together, as a hen gathers her chicks under her wings, but they were not willing (Matt. 23:37).

We can see the same sin in most of the people who were allowed to be a part of those great experiences at Möttlingen. Most of them were reassured and happy after they received what benefitted them. They thought their rejoicing over what they had received was in itself a worship service. They thought they had done enough, since they felt so happy. But such behavior gives God a raw deal. It is impossible for his kingdom to be fully effective on earth because this carnal selfishness has taken root on the soil of grace and vaunts nothing but itself.

Beyond Personal Piety

THE ABOVE POINT BECAME CRITICAL as time went on for the movement at Möttlingen. From the very beginning, even in all the joy during the great experiences, my father felt something was missing. An unspoken uneasiness made him apprehensive for the future. He was well aware that the revival movement, as thorough and extensive as it was, was only a preparation for a greater goal. But probably he himself was influenced to make the mistake of asking, "How can this movement benefit the [state] church?" Or possibly, "How can it benefit Pietism?" He might even have wondered, "How can it benefit the many people I see leading such miserable lives?" So he also tried to adjust the high waves of the movement to fit with the ideas of his time, with the traditional forms of the Christian faith and lifestyle. He was only able to stick up for one thing, and that often with a pounding heart. Wherever he went and no matter who opposed him, he insisted that we have fallen away from the great apostolic testimony that Jesus Christ will be victorious through our prayer and the power of the Holy Spirit. Therefore, he insisted that we should have our eyes fixed expectantly on a new outpouring of the Holy Spirit. He did not fully understand that this Spirit from on high is too pure, too holy, for God to pour it into only partially cleansed vessels. As long as the main focus of the Christian world was centered on "What benefits can I get from God, Christ, and the Holy Spirit?" it most certainly was not a clean enough vessel to receive greater gifts and powers. Only where people can say, "I no longer live, but Christ lives within me!" (Gal. 2:20) – "I am not interested in benefits for myself but for the Father, in Jesus Christ" – only in such people will the Holy Spirit make his dwelling, purifying their bodies and souls and glorifying the Father through the Son present in them.

This is the attitude we need to have for a people to come into being in Christ, a people made up of members who are truly useful servants to God on this earth, servants who forget themselves, servants who receive what is given to them only for their Lord's sake, who utilize what they have received solely for their Lord's profit and to his honor. Unfortunately, this reason for conversion and forgiveness of sin was lost on the Möttlingen congregation. Only a small flock, a remnant, kept a burning thirst for God and were not content to relax in God's mercy. This explains why the wonderful movement at Möttlingen, this fount of a living connection with God, did not have a world-shaking impact but disappeared again into the sand.

Christ's victory for God's cause continued to work in just a few. Christ's victory created unassuming warriors in these few. Thanks to them, we did not lose all connection to that display of God's grace. Over the years I have become more and more fully convinced that as Christians we have to completely forsake any form of self-seeking. We should consider God's justice and hunger and thirst for his righteousness (Matt. 5:6, 6:33). We should hope for God's intervention on behalf of his coming kingdom. Meanwhile we should run with perseverance the race marked out for us and throw ourselves into the fight – the fight against our own flesh. I am well aware that we have not yet resisted to the point of shedding our blood against the sin that so easily entangles us and makes us weary (Heb. 12:1–4). I feel it is a serious sin that the works of God were dwarfed because of the self-centeredness of the people to whom they were given. In any case we see our guilt here and want to accept the consequences, including God's judgment. God's mercies could lift us out of the sorry state Christianity is in today, but I am sure there is no point in thinking we will receive any more mercies until we can accept the whole of God's truth and the whole of his righteousness into our personal lives. This may well smash our self-esteem. Our self-love must be broken and we must seek God without any selfish motives before he alone can come and rule in us.

Serving Jesus Christ Alone

EVEN THOUGH GOD SOMETIMES lets us experience great grace and many blessings in order to coax us to repent (Rom. 2:4), we do not want to be numbered among those who fancy that the whole point is our own salvation. Receiving forgiveness and happiness is not the most important thing, especially if it only leads to selfishness. Today God may well be telling us: "I am going to give my truth and my righteousness more weight by judging your flesh. Up until now I have met you with grace and salvation, but you used it all selfishly. So now I will draw near in judgment, and you should come to me looking for righteousness. Then everything else will come to you of its own accord. You will not need to worry about your salvation."

This is a change in direction that I hope we can make, a different perspective based on what we learned in Möttlingen and Bad Boll. I do not think those experiences are worn-out bygones. On the contrary, they have eternal value, and they still carry us forward to this very day. But today they no longer spur us on to find happiness for people. They no longer prompt us to seek for the kingdom of God in order to make people happy. Instead they challenge us to look for who Jesus Christ really is – at the expense of our own flesh. They challenge us to examine ourselves to find out how we have disgraced God in spite of all our Christianity. We thirst for truth and righteousness. Our great delight should be to acknowledge the living God and his justice in all the blessings he gives to us. Then God's promises, given in his laws and commandments, will become more important to us than they were before. Today we can see God's kingdom sparkling in its Sabbath Day, stretching again over all of creation and establishing justice and truth. That is what we are looking forward to today, whereas before we were more or less just looking forward to bringing people to salvation. That will happen, too, but only after we have acknowledged God's claim to the whole of creation.

A New Orientation in Life

WHEN WE TOOK UP this battle against our own flesh, we found ourselves developing new orientations in life. I think they show that we had become warriors for God's kingdom. These orientations are determined by sayings of the Savior in their true sense. To evaluate a person we no longer ask whether or not he is a Christian. Instead, we ask whether or not he makes room in his life for the truth and authority of God. We ask whether he says, "Lord, Lord" (Matt. 7:21; Luke 6:46) just to smooth-talk his way into heaven, or if he really wants to do the will of the Father and is willing to die in order that Jesus may live. Moreover, if we want to know whether or not someone is sincere in his faith, we do not ask if he prays but what he prays for. If he prays only for himself, in order to get better or to feel saved through the grace of God, then we say, "You are not praying the way Jesus taught us to. You may be on your knees for hours, but test yourself. What is most important in your prayer? Is it your own dear ego, which is feeling harassed? Is that why you are calling on the Lord as if you have to shake him out of sleep so he can help you? And when you receive help, are you content? Or is God's kingdom and his righteousness most important for you?" To pray for your ego does not make you devout. You will be a true, devout believer in the biblical sense only if you are seeking for the kingdom of God – only if you are looking for help for your body and soul purely to bring forth fruit for the kingdom of God.

Besides this, we do not just look for whether a Christian is zealous. Anybody can be zealous, but what are you zealous for? Are you zealous just for your faith as opposed to the faith of others? Zealous for the programs and efforts you are working on? Think about it. Maybe you are being zealous more for yourself than for the kingdom of God. Selfishness and ambition can so easily be the ulterior motives behind our Christian zeal, causing us to turn like violent beasts against anyone who thinks differently.

This is the change of focus that I hope we can make after all we have experienced. And this is what many people have not been able to understand about us in recent years. Sorry, but we cannot help it – this is what we live and breathe today. All our thoughts and hopes are centered on finding out what it means to die with Christ, not so that we live but so that he lives (Phil. 3:10). Yes, so that his cause comes to people's attention, to God's glory, even if we have to suffer pain ourselves because God will have to pass judgment on our flesh. We are trying to understand the sacrifice we owe to God (Rom. 12:1–2). A whole offering is what we would like to be able to bring to him: body, soul, and spirit, along with our whole house – in which we have made ourselves so comfortable – yes, even its Christian furnishings. We would like to give everything back into God's hands as an offering, so that freshly cleaned vessels will stand ready on earth where the living God may dwell and where Christ may reveal himself for the benefit of God's kingdom.

The Savior said, "Do not think that I have come to abolish the Law or the Prophets; I have not come to abolish them but to fulfill them" (Matt. 5:17). Offering sacrifices is part of the Law and the Prophets. Individuals draw near to God by surrendering their own self. This was totally fulfilled by Jesus, the sacrificial Lamb of God. He sacrificed his all, so that the Father in heaven would have all rights over him. Jesus did not desire to take advantage of anything on earth for himself. He gave everything to the Father in heaven. He made this sacrifice so that we would sacrifice everything, too, and keep absolutely nothing for ourselves on earth – except what we have in Christ Jesus, the risen one, to the glory of the Father. We have been told that Christ died for us, but this does not mean Christ died so that we can live in our flesh and be saved just by believing in him. Instead it means: Christ died for us so that through him we now have a way to offer ourselves with all that we are to God, through the blood of Christ, in order to be resurrected to a new life in truth and righteousness. If the blood of Jesus Christ does not bear fruit in us, it is because his sacrifice is not fulfilled in us until we sacrifice ourselves to God in him (cf. 2 Cor. 5:14–15).

The Need for Willing Sacrifice

GOD CANNOT FORCE US to make this sacrifice. In the Old Testament God did not really demand sacrifice either, but he presupposed that the people would want to offer themselves to him. Therefore, he gave them a tangible way to contribute something of themselves. He did not desire the blood of bulls and rams. Later when people brought these sacrifices and then babied themselves, when they thought that by fulfilling the sacrificial ordinances they could avail themselves of God's help, they merely deluded themselves. They should have offered themselves of their own free will. They should not just have met an external command of God, but they should have internally striven freely and wholeheartedly to become a people of God. They should have sacrificed themselves body and soul to fulfill God's idea of what his people should be (1 Sam. 15:22; Ps. 51:16–18; Jer. 7:22–23; Hos. 6:6). Likewise, God will not force upon us the sacrifice we owe him. He will not use force to make us die with his Son. But he will show us the way, the truth, and the life in Jesus Christ, his Son, and wait to see if we can bring ourselves to accept the way of the blood of Christ, the way on which we must yield our flesh to him by dying (cf. Rom. 8:17; 2 Tim. 2:11–13). This is the only way we will recognize the full truth, and then experience eternal life and the resurrection.

So I feel that what is most important for us, after we have been given to know Jesus Christ, is that we strain every nerve not first and foremost to get into heaven but to meet God's expectations by dying to our flesh in order to bring him the offering we owe him. Of course, many people bring offerings, but they only offer what doesn't cost them much. They only offer what they have no use for anymore. Few sacrifice themselves.

Take for example an alcoholic. The lust of his flesh drives him to drink. He is not able to sacrifice this craving of his flesh as long as drinking is enjoyable. However, when he gets sick from it, then he is repulsed by his craving for alcohol and he gladly offers it to God. Another person tells lies because they get him what he wants. He knows quite well that it is wrong, but as long as he profits by lying he will not sacrifice himself and the profit for the sake of honesty and truth. But when his dishonesty is detected and he has to suffer the consequences, such as being taken to court, then certainly his selfish behavior disgusts him. Now he wishes he would have given it up. Someone else may have got sucked into a wrong spiritual direction. His waywardness has gained him prestige and honor; he has influence and power. He knows full well that not everything is right, but he can't bring himself to admit the truth and say, "I am wrong." The spiritual advantages to his position are too appealing. But if it becomes public, when he stands incriminated, then of course he would like to give up his spiritual pride, for now it has lost its appeal. Or take a person who lives happily day after day. He is religious, but thinks no further than his own life and his own comforts. His sins don't weigh him down. He is healthy and lives in good circumstances. He doesn't sacrifice anything, because he likes everything the way it is. But then he gets old and slowly his strength wanes. Now he is on his deathbed. He realizes how little he did for God in this world. Oh, yes! Now his life seems hollow to him, and he wishes he would have offered his whole life to God. But his life is over and gone. Now he can no longer be the servant he could have been if he had offered his life to God earlier. And so we see that many people offer only what they don't want. They sacrifice to their dear God what amounts to rotten eggs. But whatever they can use for their own well-being, they will not part with.

Mark this well: we have decided to fight against this innate laziness of our flesh in order to win many people, if possible, who are ready to make real sacrifices in good time – in short, people who will die so that Jesus may live. Then he will destroy the life of our flesh through his life and will work God's kingdom within us. May God create among us a people willing to sacrifice themselves, a people from whom light will radiate for all peoples. The following verse applies to such people: "Arise, shine, for your light has come, and the glory of the Lord rises upon you. See, darkness covers the earth and thick darkness is over the peoples, but the Lord rises upon you and his glory appears over you. Nations will come to your light, and kings to the brightness of your dawn" (Isa. 60:1–3).

The Battle with Ourselves

THE REASON I HAVE ELABORATED on this thought in such detail is because we realized to our great sorrow that the bright light which shone in Möttlingen during the conversions and revivals did not bear the fruits it should have borne. In spring the sunlight makes the grass and leaves grow and the buds flower, and everyone rejoices. In the same way, everyone exulted in the first signs of the kingdom of God in Möttlingen. But then in spring a bitter north wind brings frost and snow and nips the blossoms in the bud so that they do not bear fruit. In the same way, after God's display of grace, our icy egotism resisted the Father in heaven and spoiled the promise of spiritual fruit. Then the eternal life was spoiled. Then it started to look as though only after death would we find a life fit for eternity. But this pains us. With deep shame we now recognize that the icy cold blasts of egotism came from our own hearts. The North Pole that wreaked the most damage to the fruit-bringing revelations was in our own flesh!

But should we grind to a halt when faced with our flesh? Never! After all, didn't we find courage in the name of Jesus Christ to stand up against the powers of darkness and Satan? Didn't we see victories in the name of Jesus over perverse spiritual powers that wanted to engulf people? Surely we can find the courage to draw the sword against ourselves, to eradicate our egocentric Christianity, and to give God honor by gladly surrendering ourselves to the death of our flesh through the blood of Jesus Christ. When this battle is won and God's victory shines forth, then the corruption that even now is attacking masses of people who adorn themselves with the name of Jesus might be revealed and held in check. The sign of victory will be life from the risen one.

9

Beyond the Surface

IN CONNECTION WITH the spiritual movement at Möttlingen I would like to say something about the *physical healings* that followed as a result. These healings created quite a stir. People paid the most attention to them, understandably enough, but sometimes they also upset people the most. The latter was mainly because many people were attracted who were looking only for healing, without seriously asking what the requirements were for such healing. As time passed by, the character of the movement changed in this way: the stream of people developed into two streams. Some people, convicted of their sin, were looking for absolution; other people, plagued by their physical ailments, were looking for healing. A lot was given to both types of people, for the spiritual waves of the movement, at Möttlingen and later on, rose so high that even those who came more for external help were swept along for the moment – and physical improvements were often achieved more quickly than a change in their personal life.

Rumors and Exaggerations

SOON THE EXAGGERATED RUMOR spread that God's powers were helping *everybody*. "Everybody" was an exaggeration. But the rumor persisted and attracted many people, not only those selfishly concerned merely for their own souls and their own salvation, but also those who in their selfishness were interested only in their physical well-being and were satisfied when they received physical relief. It is not surprising that lies and exaggerated stories told by such self-centered people caused quite a stir – to the detriment of the whole movement. On the whole, however, the movement was respected as something holy by sincere seekers, also in regard to its benefits for people's physical well-being. God kept the healings in particular firmly in his own hands. He prevented my father from ever thinking that he could pray someone back to health. Instead, whenever sick people recovered after he had blessed them with the laying on of hands, he could only give all praise to God. Their health would improve – sometimes more, sometimes less, sometimes slowly, and sometimes surprisingly fast. The only mistake my father may have made (which I've mentioned already) is that he had so much compassion for everyone that when someone didn't receive healing, it hurt him more than necessary.

True Healing

THE FOLLOWING IDEA has simply taken root in our Christianity and become ingrained in our flesh and blood. People think the most important aspect of the kingdom of God is that God always helps *people*, be it physically or spiritually. Whereas today we say: The most important aspect of God's kingdom is that *God* receives his claim over our lives. God's first goal is not our salvation or our physical well-being but his righteousness – the rest will follow of its own accord (Matt. 6:33). That God's true nature finds room within humanity – that is what we should fix our eyes on. Before God, a healthy person is someone who is righteous and honors God and his righteousness, even if he is still suffering from spiritual or physical afflictions. Yes, before God a suffering person is often healthier than a person who looks healthy to us, because in the eyes of God a *righteous* person is already healthy. Physical recovery *may* follow – but it also may not follow immediately, because death has not yet been fully overcome.

The reports in the Gospels may have caused some misunderstanding in this respect. Being concise, they primarily praise God, who does wonders. They describe in broad strokes how Jesus "healed all" who came to him (for example, Matt. 4:23, 8:16; Luke 4:40; Acts 10:38). All? In this connection I would like to say that "healthy" means the same thing for Jesus as it does for his Father. It means "righteous," "reconciled," "redeemed from the curse of sin." Surely the first question Jesus asked a sick person was not, "What is your affliction?" but, "What is your sin?" (Matt. 9:2). When the patient's condition was such that his sin could be forgiven – whether it was secret and unnoticeable, or lurid and obvious – then he could be healed. But if his inner state was wrong, he remained sick or was in danger of becoming sick again right away (cf. John 5:14; Matt. 12:43–45). That's why chronic illness was frequently easier to heal than, say, a sore finger, because with chronic illnesses the patient usually already has a broken spirit. On the other hand, with minor injuries the patient often still has a lot of filth to deal with that he or she has not taken seriously. When sick people came to the Savior, they soon felt something of his majesty and as a rule they broke down inwardly so that he could help them.

The Whole Will of God

EVEN FOR JESUS it was up to *God* whether or not someone was helped. Jesus did not say, "I will heal this man, because I feel sorry for him." He may often have waited anxiously to see if his Father would heal someone or not (cf. John 5:19). That is why he could also shift the praise for healings from himself by saying, "These are the works of my Father in heaven" (John 9:4). The healings bore witness not that Jesus was a skilled physician but that God was with him (John 9:31). Apparently many sick people were not healed (Mark 6:5–6), and many may even have received a good scolding (Luke 4:23–27). How else can we explain why, in spite of the many healings, so much evil gossip spread, especially about his miracles of healing? Likely the Pharisees were informed by some very disgruntled people who had not received from Jesus what they wanted, who had had to turn away from him shamefaced, and who then later blasphemed against Jesus, calling everything a hoax. Jesus had to put up with being called an ordinary sorcerer (Mark 3:22–30). There is a gap in the Gospels' coverage that I would boldly like to fill in. We do not want to disgrace the Savior by letting people think he would have cured someone without considering their inner state just to draw attention to his role as a miracle worker! Then the person who was healed could have continued their sinful lifestyle and this would have dishonored God.

To think like this would be the worst insult to Jesus. Of course, there are Christians today, too, who would like to call on Jesus the way you quickly call on a doctor when something hurts. Many people think you just have to pray – or beg and carry on – until the Savior, who might be sleeping, wakes up. Then, even if he only stirs, you will be made well again. I repeat: this is an insult to the Savior. As a result, in both ancient and modern times, certain prayers have been used by Christians superstitiously like magic formulas to heal the sick without any consideration of their inner condition. The magic formula in itself was supposed to have an effect, or a picture, or a cross, or some heathen ritual. Without giving God any credit, people just wanted the sick to be healed. Even pious people had this mindset, and many still do. Many people want the sick to recover through prayer, without giving any recognition to God's honor and his claim. But if we want to avoid insulting our Savior, we have to insist that he is more concerned about the *justness* of a person than their physical health, and therefore he gave it priority.

Of course, Jesus may well have healed someone so as to give people an indication of God's authority and God's mercy, so as to draw them closer to his kingdom by showing them God's kindness (Rom. 2:4). And even if he could heal many people without further ado, we must not be misled by the idea that he healed solely out of compassion. It is simply a fact that many people are tormented by diseases and demons through no fault of their own. These may frequently have been healed just by listening to the sermons of the Savior or the apostles without anybody else noticing it. Because health is the outward sign of the inner reconciliation and forgiveness of sin (cf. Ps. 103:3), we can use the term "healthy" when we mean "justified," "reconciled with God," or "delivered from sin and the dominion of darkness."

This is certainly how it was in the beginning. Later on, Christians did not take it so seriously, and instead of going to the root of the condition, they looked more at the outer symptoms. Therefore, as with so many other things influenced by religious pressures, questions of health became a physical issue instead of remaining a spiritual issue. But this could bring down disaster on many, because by using spiritual powers for physical gains, new diseases could even come into being that no one had ever heard of before.

Forms, Methods, and Signs

AT THIS POINT I would like to commend my father's tact: he never let any method or set form of words become the norm for prayer or for the laying on of hands – because he was afraid it would be misused. He feared nothing more than superstition, like a mechanical use of even the nicest words or Bible verses. Therefore, he also placed no significance for our present day on scripture passages that speak of anointing with oil (Mark 6:13; James 5:14). In those days [Bible times], anointing with oil was used first of all as a symbol of inner purification, but secondly as a medication for the common and distressing skin diseases. At that time, oil was a normal remedy, and if prayer was offered with it, it was in the sense of the apostle Paul's words, "Whatever you do, whether in word or deed, do it all in the name of the Lord Jesus" (Col. 3:17), and "Whether you eat or drink or whatever you do, do it all for the glory of God" (1 Cor. 10:31). Later on this anointing with oil became a superficial form, and today I'm afraid its use borders on witchcraft.

I want to tell you about something that happened in Württemberg. The highly respected and pious founder of Korntal, Hoffmann,[1] once had the idea, both to honor God and as a sign for the brethren, to have small silver medallions made, imprinted with the name "Jehovah." But then we came across instances where these small medallions were worn as amulets to avert sickness. I mention this only to show how careful we have to be with the use of external things. Even the host (the consecrated communion bread) or the water from a baptismal font is frequently used in a superstitious manner. Such activity causes more harm to the soul than we are aware of. The actual power of God could flow down to us through the name of Jesus if we would regard righteousness as the best good health. But it stands to reason that God's power withdraws when we put our faith in superstition and misuse God's will to get our human, carnal, or satanic desires.

In Möttlingen, too, the danger of looking just at the surface of things was great. Not that my father ever wanted people to be healed only externally. The people came in droves, and it cannot be denied that great numbers of them were only looking for physical health. For this reason there was bound to be a setback. This superficial attitude – when someone wants to employ God for just a moment to take care of all sorts of physical or emotional maladies – can actually amount to a punishable misuse of the name of God. It can lead to mental derangement with serious consequences. In Möttlingen we had the strange experience that some people received physical healing as a result of the forgiveness of their sins and absolution, but even though their consciences were pacified through the forgiveness of sin, certain evils, certain deep curses, were not loosed. There were some cases like this at the very beginning and more and more later on.

The conversion of the whole congregation at Möttlingen enabled God to work certain signs and wonders, and these showed that a person's life had been fully freed from the clutches of death. Möttlingen really was a light demonstrating the wonderful works of God, and this light should continue to burn until the great Day dawns. But just as this light did not arise without a battle against sin, so the Day of Jesus Christ, which will conquer *all* evils, will not arise without a battle against the flesh (which lends a hand to death). We would be fooling ourselves if we thought: now

---

1 Gottlieb Wilhelm Hoffmann (1771–1846) was the leader at the Korntal community from 1820 to 1846. The elder Blumhardt had been a friend of his son Wilhelm (1806–1873) since his time at seminary. See Zündel, 15–18; 22–23; 24. About amulets see Johann Christoph Blumhardt, *Der Kampf in Möttlingen*, I, 2, 13.

that God has performed a few signs and miracles it's a done deal and all we need to do is pray and anything will be possible. Oh no, we have to meet certain requirements. Paul writes in his Letter to the Philippians that he does not consider himself to have attained the goal at which *everything* is possible, even though he feels he is on the path on which already a great deal is possible (Phil. 3:12–13). If we continue to surrender ourselves to God, to go the way of the cross of Christ, to faithfully die to our flesh with Christ, then by virtue of Christ's resurrection we can expect to see the signs to prove that *everything* is under God's control until the time when our lowly bodies will be transformed so that they will be like his glorious body (Phil. 3:2; cf. 1 Cor. 15:25–28).

10

Both Body and Soul

THE WHOLE THRUST OF THE MOVEMENT at Möttlingen was an advance toward God's kingdom and his righteousness. Through that, everything else was given – it emerged of its own accord – including restored health. But as we have seen in previous chapters, a stream of people with selfish motives, desires of the flesh, joined the crowd. They wanted to get well *first*, as if you could enter the kingdom of God automatically through a "miracle." This I admit openly, but on the other hand I must say that the church authorities demonstrated a gross misunderstanding of divine order and the laws of nature (and a total ignorance of the progress of God's kingdom on earth, in particular an ignorance of the ministry of Jesus and his disciples) when they told my father he should "stick to religion, just comfort people and tell them about the blessing of suffering and the value of patience." In other words, he should refer people exclusively to human help, as far as doctors are able to provide it, and away from any hope of God's help for physical ailments.

A God-Given Law

IT IS A GOD-GIVEN LAW of nature that *body and soul belong together* – if you are trying to help the one, you also have to consider the other. To separate body and soul is manslaughter. Passionate treatment of the body by itself can kill the soul and trample on the soul's God-given rights. On the other hand, spiritual counsel by itself can damage the body's God-given rights. Unfortunately, this has frequently happened. Any observant person can see that the practice of the church has developed in such a way that a pastor is not used to asking questions about anything except a person's spiritual state. This is doing a great deal of damage to the kingdom of God. Today a "spiritual" counselor is painfully aware that he is in effect excluded as soon as a physical need is addressed, be it political, social, or medical. We have gotten used to bypassing the church in all important questions; we think, "The church caters only to the soul."

A society is sick when care for a person's spiritual needs is totally separated from care for his or her physical needs. We could also say a society is sick when religion – separated from the realities of life – lives and moves in a world of its own. Under such separate care, people's souls will starve to death if their bodies do not render forceful assistance. Conversely their bodies will languish if their soul and spirit are not [integrated] in [the care of] their physical life. Many people are starving these days, some physically and some spiritually. That is why sometimes a person suddenly has to be admitted to a facility for physical health care without regard to their previous experiences and irrespective of whether the place will consider their spiritual needs or not. It is simply a quick solution to a physical problem. Or it can happen the other way around, that a person's physical well-being has to be disregarded, even jeopardized, in order to rescue him or her emotionally from some unhappy, shattering experience. In both cases the poor creature has already been corrupted: God's true order has already been broken.

When people are whole human beings – not mutilated either physically or spiritually – their body and soul depend on each other, and when they get sick, both body and soul will have to be considered during their recovery. Just ask any sensible doctor who has success with his patients whether he can function fully without treating the patient's inner life. Or ask any good pastor if he can help certain patients by sheer spiritual counseling without giving the body due attention, be it by a doctor or some other sensible care.

Beyond a One-Sided Approach

THE SCRIPTURES INDICATE to us in many places that body and soul are interrelated. In no Bible story is deliverance a one-sided affair. When Israel is set free inwardly, spiritually, through faith in God, then outward deliverance follows as a matter of course. God's "spiritual counselors," his anointed "ministers" – that is, the prophets and apostles – were just as much concerned for the external life and health of the nation and individual people as for the right attitude of heart toward the true God. Yes, God's commandments can almost be viewed as health regulations. If you observe them, you will be healthy. If you don't, you will get sick. God wants a healthy nation, not a sick one – a nation that lives long, not one subject to every contingency of death. In essence, that is why God gives us his laws and commandments. That's why illnesses, accidents, and all kinds of physical privation are blamed on a disregard for God's commandments. The priests of Israel were given special instructions on how to treat many physical illnesses. And it was naturally expected of the prophets to work miracles for the poor and sick people, as well as to give help and advice for physical life in general. God wants our inner life to be made right through his commandments, and then from our inner life will come the reason and *the gift* of good care for the body. In *this* sense it is written: "I am the Lord, who heals you" (Exod. 15:26). That means, "I give you both the rules for good health and the medicines for good health."

What was given to the priests and prophets was perfected in the person of Jesus Christ. He brought the spiritual life and the physical life *together* before God. From God's hand, he carried within himself the authority to care for both. Take note that no matter what we quote from scripture about care for the body, physical healings, great miracles, or even the raising of the dead, every instance is grounded not only in the physical realm but in the psychological and spiritual realm as well. For the ministering caregivers were not simply physicians, but men of God and prophets, as were Jesus and his apostles. Consequently, we, as followers of Jesus (or shall we say as spiritual counselors), have even more right to take notice of the body than, in reverse, the physicians have the right to counsel spiritually – unless they are people of God at the same time.

The impact of the spiritual on the physical is obvious everywhere in scripture. That is probably why people who represent a certain scientific approach turn away from the idea almost in disgust, and for the same reason they don't want to hear anything about demons. They think the body should do everything for the soul, whereas they deny the soul any chance to help the body. But you can say "a healthy soul produces a healthy body" just as well as saying "a healthy body contains a healthy soul." The second is wrong in any case, if we consider "healthy" to mean "righteous." Of course, for those who do not care whether their inner life is righteous or not – that is, those interested only in the immediate satisfaction of their animal needs – a healthy body may be all they desire in this world. But sooner or later their life will turn out all wrong. Their body will eventually break down and the uneasiness in their soul will be exposed all the more, to their shame, because their inner life is corrupt. On the other hand, divinely led people, who pay attention to the health of their whole person and above all to their inner being, will also in time break down physically, but we do not need to feel sorry for them. These words of Jesus will be fulfilled for them, "The one who believes in me" – or who becomes righteous in me – "will live, even though they die" (John 11:25–26).

Jesus: Doctor and Counselor

Jesus is the prime example, both in word and deed and for all the world to see, that the physical and the spiritual *cannot be separated*. He is, in his own person, the original pattern of body and soul being in each other and for each other and with each other. So for him the separation of body and soul – death – was unnatural. In regards to his ministry to others, as the Savior he is just as much an example of a *doctor* with divine power as a *spiritual counselor* with divine power. According to the point of view of the church authorities who prohibited my father from concerning himself with people's physical needs, Jesus would have had to separate the physical and spiritual interdependence – he would have had to "just comfort people and tell them about the blessing of suffering and the value of patience." But why then did the Savior perform the greatest *physical* miracles? Certainly not because he just liked to perform miracles – incomprehensible and unfathomable miracles – but because he could reestablish the deep, divine order within human beings, according to which body and soul belong together, and because he worked only on the basis of this divine order within nature. Take note: he worked from the inside to the outside, not the other way around. He was the greatest doctor because he was the greatest counselor – not the greatest counselor because he was the greatest doctor. In Jesus' presence, first of all the inside was cleansed and the inner life healed; then, sometimes on its own, sometimes through appropriate prayers, the physical was put in order as well. Before the hidden majesty of the Savior, people's untruthful, rebellious inner lives, which had led them into immoral practices and unhealthy lifestyles, broke down. Repentance turned out to be a wellspring of truth and life. The truth brought a freeing, also for the body and physical health. That's why nothing was easier for the Lord Jesus than to speak a life-giving word, through which the name of his Father was visibly glorified in someone's body.

Modern Medicine and Inner Help

THE CURRENT TREND (which started long ago and is spreading) to separate [care for] the body from [care for] the soul is no proof that it is right – even though, unfortunately, in more and more cases they really do have to be separated. Rather, it is proof of how warped and uneven the ground on which we stand has become from the bottom up, so that people's growth is bound to be stunted either physically or spiritually. No wonder that medical science as such is flourishing and has gained such power in our time. But this does not prove that spiritual counselors should have nothing to do with the physical well-being of people. It just shows that they have paid too little attention to people's physical needs because they considered it to be outside their sphere of ministry and duty. Since the physical is just as important as the soul, God did not want people to physically waste away just because of the one-sidedness of his servants who did not care about people's physical needs. So God let it happen that medical scientists did their utmost to get the body under their control. This is why scientists made greater advances in their realm than those called originally to be counselors did in theirs. Especially when people researching the body had a straightforward, honest approach, it was easy for God to let them make discoveries for the physical life. I have often noticed that it is not so much scientific knowledge as a certain sensitivity for the laws of nature that releases healing powers, which then can benefit thousands of people.

So counselors who deal exclusively with emotional problems are marginalized because in most cases their ministry is so delicate, incomprehensible, and removed into ethereal space that you cannot grasp it. This is not the way it should be. Take the example of the Savior. It is precisely under the care of a spiritual counselor that we should see the most tangible, visible, physical changes and new life. We still also need caregivers for the body for the many sudden disorders in human life. But doctors can't make a decision over life and death – only God can do that. The warden of the body has similar responsibilities to a railroad warden: he has to see that the rails for the life of the body are kept free and open. He might have to remove a branch from the tracks here or a boulder there. Or he has to report immediately to the higher-ups any bigger interference or danger to the rail system. But he is not the engineer of the train or the stationmaster. He cannot shout "Stop!" or "Go!" as he likes. These decisions are assigned to a higher command. So we also cannot say, "This is for the doctor – that is for God!" as has been the slogan recently; just as we cannot say, "This is for the soul – that is for the body!" without causing great injury. Such slogans don't come from God but from our own selfish, perverse lives and ideas – derailed from the natural order of God.

11

Who Has the Last Word?

THE CHURCH AUTHORITIES QUASHED my father's efforts to help people who were sick in body. He was striving to work for the kingdom of God, but they felt he was not authorized for it. Even though I am saddened by this, I will let the subject rest as less important and rather discuss my father's attitude to the protests of the church authorities. After all, my father's business is our business, too, and his mistakes affect us as well. So we have to recognize them and openly confess them. It will not hurt my father nor dim the light of his godly ministry. On the contrary, by openly confessing his mistakes, which have hovered over that light like dark shadows, and by judging ourselves along with him, we are trying to eliminate the shadows so the light can shine with pristine clarity. I cannot imagine my father being angry with me for acknowledging his faults. I think he would encourage me. He did not care about himself or his person, so I will not worry about that either. I intend to serve the Lord Jesus and the cause of truth only, just as he did. If, therefore, the shell of human error is peeled away and destroyed, setting free the kernel of God's truth, I know my father would also rejoice.

My Father's Failure

I DO NOT DENY that my father was sometimes too obedient in deference to others, more obedient than was right before God. This is true in regard to the instructions referred to previously, given by the church authorities at that time. Even though he held to his convictions privately – and had to – he still thought he should comply in public. He failed to hand down to us an open declaration for the world to see, and above all for the church. As a result, the impact of his work for physical healing could be ignored by the world at large even though he held to it in private. Of course, my father justified his outward obedience as a matter of courtesy. But if something is justified by superficial human reasoning that does not mean it is justified before God – at least not in its main points. My father was well aware of his rights before God, and he was no less aware of the injustice done to him. But he didn't speak up. When he finally felt forced to speak up, he did not talk to the right people or with the necessary discretion. So, instead of benefitting the cause, it was detrimental. He should have told the church authorities right at the beginning: "You are not standing on the right foundation, and I cannot follow your lead. If I did, we would all fall into a pit. The cause of God's kingdom is too important for me – so I cannot honor what you say." Sadly, in his obedience to the church and its representatives, as well as to his brothers and friends, he allowed himself to be influenced so much that it seemed to him to be just as important to be a "good boy" to these brothers and the church authorities as to stay true to his cause.

An indication of how long my father tried to please his brothers and the church authorities is given by his extended dependency on the Calw Publishing House for his work as an author. In those days, Dr. Barth[1] edited and slashed my father's frequently very original essays that pointed to God's kingdom. This often greatly pained my father. For example, in the publication of his missionary history,[2] Dr. Barth cut or weakened passages that were especially distinctive. But my father put up with it out of love for the brethren, even though God was giving him other commands. He could have and should have dared to testify to what God was calling him to. He should have testified with an inner conviction of faith without getting embroiled in open strife over superficial matters. Because he allowed himself instead to be swayed and gave way (on the surface) for the sake of peace, his usually clear insight was dulled, and things came to a standstill.

God's Kingdom or the Church?

THIS WAS A BIG MISTAKE. It made us fully realize the error we have discussed already, which had serious repercussions. My father was so

---

1 Dr. Christian Gottlob Barth, the pastor at Möttlingen preceding the elder Blumhardt, founded the Calw Publishing Association in 1833, which he directed fulltime as of 1838. Blumhardt worked intensively for this publishing house (see Zündel, 110–116) and authored important works. About his relationship with Barth, see Zündel, 103–105. Blumhardt gave regular reports to Barth regarding Möttlingen by letter. About Blumhardt finding an inner freedom from Barth, see Zündel, 153–155.

2 Johann Christoph Blumhardt, *Handbüchlein der Missionsgeschichte und Missionsgeographie* (Calw and Stuttgart: Calver Verlagsverein, 1844).

much a part of the Lutheran Church, so much at home with its laws and its whole nature, that he thought the kingdom of God could come into being only within the precepts of the established church. He thought he was duty-bound to place all his accomplishments and his most sacred moments into the bosom of the church and its representatives. He thought that if he did not make them common property for all within the church, they could not become common property for the furtherance of God's kingdom. He believed that he had to justify his actions before the church even to the smallest details and the most sacred events, although his actions were already regarded as legitimate by God. He thought experiences sanctioned by God still had to be authorized by the church in order to be truly legitimate.

To give an illustration: My father was a servant in God's kingdom; the church was the inspector. Now the servant received a commission directly from the Lord and justifiably felt obliged to inform the inspector in order to respect him at the same time. But the inspector, who long since had become used to acting at his own discretion, thought the Lord's instructions were highly impractical, unsuitable, and disruptive to his own mode of operation. So he ordered the servant to take a completely different course of action than the Lord had commanded. The servant had to obey the inspector, for it says: "Let everyone be subject to the governing authorities" (Rom. 13:1). This is how it happened that the Lord's commission was killed by the inspector, and the servant had a hard time getting back on track.

One fruit of this hard time was the written memorandum[3] that my father placed into the lap of the church authorities "as a kind of secret confessional." In it we find laborious discussions, conscientious descriptions, humble justifications, and finally the timid request to the esteemed inspector, so to speak: would he be kind enough to respect the commission given to me by the Lord himself? If the authorities had to be dealt with at all, my father should have given them a clear, straightforward statement at the right moment, even at the risk of disfavor. He should have told the inspector to submit to the Lord's commands. My father could have saved himself the effort of trying to explain his actions and make them palatable to people who still did not understand but were only strengthened all the more in their own opinion that my father had been hoodwinked.

But since he did not do this, my father was obliged to write his "defense," for better or for worse. And even in his defense he was not the free servant he should have been, but remained the obedient slave of the

---

3 Johann Christoph Blumhardt, *Krankheitsgeschichte*.

inspector – more so than was right – by limiting the boundaries of his defense to the time-honored orders and laws of the church. In his apology, his first priority was to be justified under the church: under the Augsburg Confession, the Catechism, and prevailing Christian good taste. Only as a second priority did he dare to timidly indicate the commission he had received from the Lord. He tried to fit this commission – which was something new – into the old framework without damaging it too much.

Obedience versus Freedom

IN THIS WAY MY FATHER sewed a patch of unshrunk cloth onto an old garment and poured new wine into old wineskins (Mark 2:21–22). This mistake caused both him and us a lot of trouble. Instead of checking the commandments of the Lord against the precepts of the church, he should have placed the Lord's commandments in center stage and used them to throw light on the precepts of the church. Jesus first – then the authorities, the church, the confession. If the latter do not agree with Jesus, then they are wrong, not Jesus. In the last analysis, who has the right to speak in the kingdom of God, to give commands and make decisions? State and church traditions or Jesus, the Lord? Is God obliged throughout all centuries to pour his kingdom's jewels into old, dead, manmade vessels, where they get damaged and corrupted? It is about time we give up the idea! How could the Lord Jesus be shoehorned into any one of the many churches and sects planted by man throughout time? How could God choose just that one to bless the world? We would be left anxiously wondering which one he is selecting for himself.

We have to acknowledge that the almighty God in Jesus will need more space and more free reign than those churches can give who think they offer salvation (or even that they alone offer salvation). Jesus does not let himself become involved in church arguments. His kingdom arches high above everything else, just as it once spanned over fossilized Judaism. We do not want to fight selfishly and dogmatically for our own interests as the Pharisees once did. I think such selfishness is the greatest obstacle for the kingdom of God and should be thrown into the consuming fire of the one and only true God. We do not want to claim anything as our own anymore. We have nothing by which we can show off and say, "I am better than you! My faith brings salvation – yours does not!"

No, let us rather shake hands freely as brothers. Let us be one group, ready for sacrifice. Let us stand before God and say, "Here we are – foolish, poor, wretched, blind, and naked! We know we are nothing and you are all in all! So we do not want anything for ourselves anymore, but everything only for you and your kingdom. We want to be your true children. Put into our hands your tools so that we can serve in your kingdom on earth." This way of humility and self-sacrifice is the only way we can still turn into a people God can use. Then he can supply us with strength to help people to find renewal in body and soul, to overcome sickness and death.

Loving God above All

LET US HEAD TOWARD this goal! Oh, that our hearts would be on fire! I do not mean with the "Christian" love for our neighbor that kowtows to the flesh at the expense of God's truth and righteousness. Oh, that we would catch on fire with the *love of God* that sacrifices itself – that strives to serve only God and his kingdom and that unites with the same longing in our neighbor. In this love let us join hands in covenanted fellowship. This love, agape, is the love the Savior and the apostles knew, and actually practiced. We, too, must get to know the inner character of this love. The ultimate harmony of humanity and the whole of creation is unthinkable without this divine love, which is a gift of God (cf. Rom. 8:19–23). Under the banner of this divine love, all nations will finally and easily unite as brothers and sisters. They will know no barriers created by human religiosity or party politics. United under this banner of God, they will rejoice in the wonderful freedom of being children of God, and they will help to build up Zion – the Zion that God wants to establish on this earth.

As you can see from the presentation above, we have adopted a *new* spiritual standpoint. As a result, we have been exposed to a veritable storm of chatter. It surrounded us like a whirlwind and would have blown away the whole of Bad Boll if it could have.[4] We simply had to make up for what my father had sidestepped. Because he wanted to spare himself any critique from seriously thinking Christians, he accommodated himself to them in Christian love. By the end nearly everyone was pleased with him. At least they were satisfied that "despite his peculiarities" he could be considered a defender of the church and Christendom in general.

We are different today. In fact, wherever we go we hear people saying, "How things have changed at Bad Boll!" The most atrocious rumors get linked to people's anger. People are angry because we dare to insist that our

---

4 See W. Jäckh, *Blumhardt: Vater und Sohn und ihre Welt*, 134ff. In 1894, Christoph Blumhardt decided to discontinue church customs in Bad Boll. He also turned just as sharply against the trend that for every case of illness we must simply pray for healing. About this see E. Jäckh, *Christoph Blumhardt*, 126ff., 130ff.

love to God places Christian love for our neighbor in second place. From this new standpoint, we see much that is not right, both with ourselves and with our traditional Christian practices.

Please do not think that we are out to insult anyone. And please do not think that we have come to our present position by critiquing human relationships. It is not because we have recognized the mistakes my father may have made that we take a different position than my father. Rather, it is because of a new insight into the truth and the righteousness of God. Since God has opened our eyes to our previous mistakes, we feel called to be zealous for God's truth and righteousness whether it suits us or not. Just because the judgment that came to us and our community crossed over our precincts and others felt struck with us – and got angry – is no proof that we are wrong or that we intended to hurt Christian love of neighbor. (By the way, as painful as it was, we felt a certain satisfaction in being judged by the truth for God's sake.) It does prove, however, how deeply sunk we were in the waters of conventional Christian sentiments. And so we could not see any way to change ourselves without bringing pain to the circles around us. By trying to target ourselves, we also hit them. Does that mean we should be silent? No! We have committed ourselves as a group no longer to fight in the first place for ourselves or for Christian love, but only for God's love, for agape. In agape, we consider the rights and truths of God first, before we give any thought to our personal wishes. The following verses are for this committed group. These verses came from my ardent desire for a reorganization of all things under agape on behalf of the kingdom of God.

A Song of Agape

Rise up, children of the Father!
Come with joy, your bond renew.
Gathered in a holy hour,
You've made a vow both firm and true.
Rise, and see the light from heaven,
Shining from the Lord above.
In the hour of death and darkness,
He will send us life and love.

Would you wander in the desert
As God's people did of yore?
Many miles they had to cover,
Barely finding Canaan's shore.

They were deaf to God's voice calling,
Disregarded his commands.
So the Lord in wrath appalling
Struck them down in barren lands.

Do not fear the light and clearness
Coming from God's holy face.
He is faithful, true, and righteous.
He is justice crowned with grace.
Do not murmur when his judgment
Stings or burns your human pride.
When your selfish flesh is broken,
God is honored in your stride.

He will lead you – straight the pathway
To the goal, the promised land.
Fear of death and dreadful nightmares
Flee away at his command.
Mark, your longings must be selfless
To escape temptations' threats.
Let your love grow strong and stronger:
Love alone can conquer death.

Seek that love which sacrifices,
Giving all to meet God's goal –
This requires your utmost service.
Then new life will fill your soul.
Turn from fleeting earthly pleasures!
Dare to walk a holy path!
You will find love is eternal.
Love alone will always last.

Love is power, love is victor.
Love came here from heav'n to dwell.
Love has broken man's last terror,
Overcoming death and hell.
Love – her love on earth bestowing
From on high, from God's own breast –
Comes to bring us joy o'erflowing.
Glory falls upon the blessed.

Love proclaims her God, her Master,
From whose heart she comes to men –
Kindles fires the whole world over,
Blazing up to God again.
Blazing up to be re-nourished
At the throne of thrones on high,
Love descends to deepest regions
God's great power to glorify.

Love can see and feel creation
Groaning for her breath of peace.
Love unites the warring nations –
Zion's hill they climb with ease.
Every knee shall bow together:
Love makes equal, love makes free.
Heav'n and earth embrace each other
In the kingdom's jubilee.

Gathered as a holy people,
Seek this love to be your guide.
All the doors that once were bolted,
Touched by love will open wide.
You were called by love, commissioned
To a bond of holiness.
So when enters God's own kingdom,
With his holiest you'll be blessed.

PART IV

The Forward Advance

Hope and the Coming Kingdom

12

Sources of Hope

THE NEXT STEP in presenting the development of our present standpoint forces us to take note of another spring from which my father drank deeply. The living water from this spring vitalized this man so noticeably in all of his battles that we can freely say that a breath of life from the Savior encompassed him, which gripped everyone in his vicinity to a greater or lesser degree. He became well known not only because he had battled with darkness; not only because his congregation, which had been languishing in superstition, was resurrected and cleansed through the mercy of the forgiveness of sin; not only because of the healings, which we have discussed in previous chapters; but also because of his bold hopes. What Christ said to the Samaritan woman: "Whoever drinks the water I give them will never thirst" (John 4:14) was fulfilled for my father particularly in reference to his hopes. In my father we witnessed a man who in spite of all his insight into human misery and in spite of all his lamenting over his own weakness still in the depths of his soul was never thirsty – he drank from an eternal spring of remarkable hope.

Being Gripped by God

IN THIS DRINKING he was akin to all those people who – breathed on by the prophets – counted their own life as nothing compared to the great pearl of God's kingdom. Even though he had not yet obtained the prize, he was taken hold of by Jesus Christ (Phil. 3:12–14). He did not consider himself yet to have taken hold of the prize, but he was gripped by the future he glimpsed in his spirit. He pursued this goal with such ardor and with the whole of his being to such an extent that even his most intimate friends were taken aback. A man once told me that my father was the only entirely biblical man he knew. This man was a theologian. My father was gripped precisely by the incomprehensible in scripture – better said, not in scripture but in the spiritual lives of the prophets and the apostles who gathered around Christ – the incomprehensible that baffles the wisdom of the wise. This is what had taken hold of him. This was the basic component of his life.

My father understood not only the nature of darkness; he understood not only the miraculous birth of Israel, on the heels of which God's deeds blossomed to the extent that the history of Israel became a history of the miraculous deeds of God; he also understood the new earth and the new heaven described by the prophets and the apostles. He understood this new heaven and new earth not only as a believer does who "believes" in something he cannot fathom. No, he *comprehended* what is involved in hoping for a new heaven and a new earth, what has to happen before a new heaven and a new earth can come into being. Gripped by this, even though he did not yet fully understand the Bible, he knew enough to know that Bible study per se will not advance the kingdom of God. Instead, he was convinced that it always depends on extraordinary powers, the powers that go forth from God, the sole creator – only God's power can bring about progress in God's kingdom. He did not formulate this point of view as clearly as we see it today, but it was dawning on him, and a lot of light broke through the dark clouds to show us that the kingdom of God is different from what has developed through human effort and taken shape in [today's] churches. God's kingdom is a creation of God. Any advances within God's kingdom are the work of God.

God's Work, Not Human Development

THAT IS WHAT WE SAY today, and we boldly cut ourselves loose from any hope that a Christian spirit will evolve through sheer human endeavors. When God created the world, he created it through spirit-filled light (Gen. 1:2–3), and when the first human became human, it happened through the life-giving breath of God (Gen. 2:7). Humanity bears the breath of God, and if this were not so we would be animals. The continuing development of humanity on this earth should have proceeded according to the nature of the first creation – through successive acts of new creation until the transfiguration of the earth. This was, this is, and this will be the kingdom of God.

The cloud of dust raised by the battle of light against darkness, the battle of the spirit against the flesh, the battle of life against death, hid this creative light from the eyes of most living beings that bore the name of human being. So virtually the whole of humankind branched out and developed only in the way animals do. As a whole, they could not understand their Creator anymore, and they had to depend on what had been created. So we could describe their religions as being like strange dances. They cavorted wildly around the powers and laws of God that they saw living in his creatures. Of course, this called for making plants and animals and people into gods – and spirits and demons. But these gods were laid low again and again – shown to be worth nothing – in comparison to even the tiniest residue of intellect that resides in every bearer of God's breath, even a pagan. Yet even this religious frenzy (of a humankind that had branched away from its Creator and become lost in worshiping created beings) must be respected as pointing toward the Creator. We should not be surprised, however, when we see those who bear witness to the kingdom of God (above all Jesus Christ) detach themselves from the mass of humanity. We are permitted to see them communing with their Creator – without any religion – freely looking up to the Father. In contrast to previous religions, Jesus said, "I and the Father are one" (John 10:30). As I have already mentioned, all men who represented God's kingdom drank from this well-spring. They did not draw strength from existing religious points of view or from existing forms of faith, but from the works of God. They believed according to their own experience of the Creator. Because of the source from which their faith flowed, their faith was reason to hope in the Creator, who alone can be truth and life for the world.

I could walk you through the length and breadth of Holy Scripture and show you how many people were drawn to God's kingdom and actively worked for God's kingdom (that is for the truth and righteousness of God's works). They were connected by a thread of hope that never died out but always broke forth again and again with new clarity. I could show you how the light broke through the darkness again and again, how the light freed devout people from the religious frenzy of the general populace and set them apart from their contemporaries, who were steeped in false hopes and superstition. I could review more explicitly how Abraham, Moses, David, Elijah, Isaiah, and Jeremiah took their cues from God's works and actively prepared the way for the coming of the Creator's Son, who perfectly portrayed the Creator's power (cf. Heb. 11:1–12:3). I could show how the attitude of all men and women of God differed radically from the attitude of other people; how they relied *solely* on strength from God, from God's kingdom; how they *never* drew strength from mere flesh (Jer. 17:5), lest they suffer a

merciless death in spite of their prophetic calling; and how we owe everything to this upright approach of the apostles and prophets. I could tell you
how enthusiastically we therefore look up to him who is not from below but
from above (John 3:31, 8:23), who must be called the Son of the living God
now and in all eternity – because for our time, too, we place our hopes on
nothing else and no one other than the Creator, as far as the kingdom of
God is concerned. But this would take too long. I'm only trying to indicate
for someone who is serious about the kingdom of God how biblical my
father really was when hope welled up within him (hope that many skeptics
looked at askance).

The Goal Stays the Same

IN LIGHT OF THESE general observations, we can look at my father's
life. Now we can see that the way he worked and lived was biblical – was
based on biblical *hope*. What differentiated him from other believers was
not his orthodoxy nor his knowledge of the Bible, not his pure character
in his relationships with people nor his gift of preaching. What brought
about his unique ministry was the hope that springs from God and leads
to his kingdom. By virtue of this hope he reached forward with his whole
being toward the same goals that (according to scripture) the prophets and
apostles were working for. The more narrowly my father focused on these
goals, the more broad-minded he had to become in regards to everything
else – everything that did not directly lead to the goal. Church ordinances,
religious traditions, and the upkeep of dogmatic regulations had to take
second place. "Be ready for changes" was the order of the day when it came
to making way for God's plans as per scripture.

We take this same approach today. In my opinion the first and most
important thing for every believer in Jesus Christ is to find out and understand clearly what the goals are that the Spirit of Christ has brought close to
us – what goals are waiting to be fulfilled through the Spirit on this visible
earth, yes, even in all God's creatures. Today we have essentially the same
hopes as my father. It is not true that he had a false interpretation of scripture and cherished unwarranted hopes. His interpretation was scriptural
according to the Spirit. So we must hope for the same things as he did. Yes,
our hope today is rooted in his. But maybe our hope is more certain, more
definite, more freed from our personal desires, and therefore has become
bolder and more far-reaching. My father was like Moses, who at the end of
his life was allowed to see the Promised Land in the distance with rather
nebulous outlines (Deut. 34:1–4). Some of the existing religious life of the

church seemed to him to be a blessing, and so he incorporated it into his hopes; he could hardly conceive of the fulfillment of the promises without it.

Now we are closer to seeing the promises fulfilled; we can see more definite outlines. Times have advanced. Today anyone who wants to can see that the old forms of the religious life people are used to are getting shaky. Many people are beginning to realize that they had better be ready to accept drastic changes even to what they hold most dear, if the kernel of the gospel is to be preserved. Now I am sure that we should not be held up in any way if a tradition breaks that we thought was a time-honored and sacred legacy of our fathers. Instead, we must focus solely on the goals of God's kingdom – set free of any human scheming – if we want to be ready to serve the kingdom of God and receive its promises. That is why some practices that my father thought were good proved to be of no use to us. In fact they were like a raging current that carried us away from the main issue and swept us into side issues. So today we diverge to some extent from my father only on *how* to reach God's goals – but the goals are the same.

13

False Staffs

THREE THEMES FROM MY FATHER'S LIFE still shine today like lodestars.[1] They also rescued him when all other lights went out. These basic themes were born in the eternal, in God himself and in his creation, and so they lead toward the eternal. Even though some of my father's ideas were human and transitory, these hopes were divine and eternal. They pointed toward the coming of God's kingdom, and without their realization the kingdom cannot come in all its fullness.

Three Hopes

ABOVE EVERYTHING ELSE, my father's calling was to plant the seeds of these hopes into the hearts of people who were hoping with him for God's kingdom to come. The three hopes that took root in him are:

Hope for a new outpouring of the Holy Spirit. The Holy Spirit is the Alpha and Omega [the beginning and the end] in humanity's development as the image of God. The Holy Spirit is the breath of God in creation, and so he is the light of life within human beings. At the end of all our struggling and developing, the Holy Spirit will be like a river of God's truth and God's righteousness leading every created thing into eternal life.

Hope for the formation of Zion. Zion is a people of God, who as a little flock (Luke 12:32) are able to receive God's kingdom in Jesus Christ, the Lord. Through the redemptive blood of Jesus Christ they will be the refuge for all peoples and nations, for both the living and the departed.

---

1 Each of three hopes listed here is developed further in a following chapter, given its biblical justification, and set against the three false supports also listed here. See also Zündel, 513–519.

Hope for death to be swallowed up (Isa. 25:8; 1 Cor. 15:54). Then God's life will break forth victoriously, and Jesus, the resurrected one, will glorify his Father on earth.

Simply by my statement of these three hopes, you will see that they differ from the views of my father's contemporaries, in fact, specifically from other believers. My father also had been taught to accept the following assertions: We believe that we have the Holy Spirit. We believe that we are Zion, the gathering place for all nations. We believe that death has been conquered. In the following, however, we will see how this faith held by the church had to be changed into hope – a fact that neither my father nor we regret. For these attributes of God's kingdom seen through the eyes of hope were the Promised Land for this man of God. He trudged relentlessly on like a pilgrim through all turmoil toward the Promised Land, even though he was not able to reach it in this life (cf. Deut. 34:1–4). For the *staffs*, the walking sticks that this brave traveler leaned on, turned out to be not as enduring as the hopes were. Even though he trusted his staffs, one after another they broke. In the end, after one last look of longing at the Promised Land, the pilgrim himself collapsed without having reached his goal.

Three False Staffs

WE HAVE TO ADDRESS the staffs that became fateful for my father, for in order to reach God's goals, we must not rely on them anymore.

For my father's *first* hope – a new outpouring of the Holy Spirit – his staff was the visible *church*, the Christian fellowship as it has come into being in religious circles. He could see that this church was not united in *one* spirit, since he was acquainted with Christendom through his many contacts in various Christian countries. But still the current church life, as shaped by history, was sacred for him, and it was inconceivable to him that God might pour his Spirit into any other vessel. He invested an incredible amount of effort and perseverance in trying to tailor his hopes to fit the accustomed religious forms. He did not get discouraged but continued to hope that the church would take up his hopes and change accordingly. In spite of repeated rejection by the advocates of church forms, it did not occur to him that these *vessels* might not have *eternal* worth – that they did not have to be embraced with the same love as the Immortal One. The vessel which he held up to God with the prayer that it would be filled with the Holy Spirit did not appear to him the way it really was. In many ways the vessel was crafted by human skill and therefore was defiled. It was not worthy to receive the gift of the Holy One. His request was pleasing to God, but could not be granted for the reasons indicated above. My father's staff broke and his hope remained unfulfilled.

The *second* great hope, which my father set up like a beacon, was the hope for God's Zion, a city all nations will stream to, where they will receive righteousness and truth (Isa. 2:2–3). For this hope he relied too quickly on the staff placed quite naturally into his hand: *mission*. You may be surprised that I regard this as a staff that broke in my father's hand. He often said – and with good reason – that God had opened a door for mission during his lifetime. It was like a renewing of the Lord's command to go into all the world and make disciples of all nations (Matt. 28:19), which excited Christian circles of his time. This is certainly true. But just like in early Christian times, there was the constant danger of putting more emphasis on spreading the gospel than on building up Zion, a city in which all worldly powers are overcome, a place where the Lord himself can rule through his spirit. My father did not recognize this danger clearly enough.

Of course, in his mission circles my father did emphasize his hope for Zion, but he was little understood. In those days there was a lot of enthusiasm for mission, and on his part he made the mistake of anticipating too much help from mission for the realization of his hoped-for Zion. Yes, he grasped this staff with such energy and blind trust, in spite of various warnings (even warnings from above), that he did not realize that it could only last if at the same time God's people were strengthened inwardly through grace and revelations from Jesus Christ. God's people must be filled with eternal realities, with truth and justice, with Jesus himself. Then and then only do God's people have the right to offer themselves to all nations. True mission cannot be a human effort – it must come purely from God. I would almost say: God alone has the authority to be a missionary among the nations. As missionaries, we have authority only to open the gates of Zion for nations who have been awakened and summoned by the light of God. We are not meant to push our opinions on them or burden them with our denominations.[2]

History clearly shows that the spread of Christendom brought with it *our* national characteristics, all the historic achievements of *our* nations. We have to be careful not to thoughtlessly commend these achievements to other nations unless we simply want to Germanize, Anglicize, or Gallicize them, instead of directing them to the free truth of Christ. And so, in the enthusiasm for mission, the zeal to build up Zion was neglected – that is, the

---

2 This idea is fully detailed in Christoph Blumhardt, *Christus in der Welt: Briefe an Richard Wilhelm* (Zürich: Zwingli Verlag Zürich, 1958).

zeal to unite with others who no longer live for themselves but only for God through Jesus (cf. 2 Cor. 5:15). Therefore, as a staff for my father to reach his hope for Zion, even mission (when blessed with so much zeal) was to break in his hand. Mission was invigorating for those who were not striving to build up Zion, but for my father it turned out to be a loss – as soon became obvious. In spite of his eagerness to help the missionaries, these mission circles were not inspired by the same eagerness to incorporate his hope for Zion into their preaching of the gospel to the nations.

I also want to mention the *third* staff that broke under my father's hand: the staff to support his hope that death would be swallowed up. This staff was the striving for *personal salvation* and heavenly bliss. Even though this striving is justified, it was emphasized way beyond its merits. Devout people were consumed by the desire for *personal* happiness in heaven *after death*. They forgot to look for what *God* can give on *earth* – for the revealing of divine life in Jesus Christ for all people on earth. This overemphasis on personal salvation hangs together with the whole development of Christian churches. The quest for happiness in the other world was placed far above the hope given to us in the appearance of Jesus Christ. Since this hope for heaven, for happiness in the world above, was virtually the only reason to be devout, the flesh [our selfishness] intruded with full force into this hope. That is why Christians spent most of their efforts in light of God's kingdom aspiring for blessedness and patiently putting up with all the immoral, blasphemous conduct of this world.

My father himself definitely did keep his eyes open for the meaning of earthly events in light of the eternal. In his talks and sermons a certain confidence often emerged (sometimes more clearly than at other times) that God's life will show itself here on earth, visibly, in our physical well-being as a force opposing death, which is engulfing us everywhere. Yet somehow he had grown up so intimately attached to this staff that death seemed to him to be less a judgment and more often something holy and liberating. Everyone else also thought that if death leads to salvation, even if it is painful, it should be revered. The advantages were too attractive, and he thought that anything beneficial for people in their quest for salvation must also be beneficial for God. He underestimated the will of God to make eternal life possible *on earth*. Here, where death rules as judgment over sin, this is where Christ will nullify that judgment. Through the power of Christ's resurrection, truth and life will triumph here over death, which has infiltrated everywhere.

Death does not win victories for God – life does! Death is not holy – life is holy. Our calling and purpose are not up in heaven, in the invisible, but down here on earth, in the visible, in nature. Here, where God has put us, is where we should make way for God's kingdom to be revealed, for the life of our God to be made public. Heaven with its bliss is not our final goal! Rather, on one hand, it is the place from which we can work for eternal things on earth. And on the other hand, it may well be a place where God cares for those who through their own fault or someone else's fault did not fulfill their purpose on earth. My father realized this, too, but he could not act on it, because he was not ready to let go of the staff of personal salvation. So instead of supporting him, this staff finally broke under him: that is, he did not live to see death overcome on earth as he had hoped.[3]

---

3 In the *Vertrauliche Blätter* there follows here a postscript entitled "News," included here in its entirety: "This year I hope to write two or possibly three more booklets to follow this one, and that will complete this presentation of my current position. Then the publication of these little booklets will stop, because I think I will have said enough, that is unless some reason comes up for publishing something. For the time being, however, as I have already said, I feel that I have said enough. I would like to express the wish that you read again what has been published already. I cannot continue publishing a newspaper – it wouldn't comport with the spirit of truth, which I want to represent – because a newspaper would force me to write. I want to write only when I have some real reason for it. So I would like to ask my friends to be content with this for the time being. Please let anything you felt was true grow in your hearts until it brings forth fruit. Therefore, in the New Year, 1896, the circulation of these confidential papers will stop."

14

A New Outpouring

AFTER THESE GENERAL REMARKS about the hopes that welled up in my father's heart from the depths of his experiences of God, let us turn to these hopes themselves and my thoughts on them. The first question is: Why concern ourselves with the Holy Spirit? And connected to that: How should we respond to the hope for a new outpouring of the Holy Spirit?

Concerning the Holy Spirit

IT IS WITH GRAVE RESERVATIONS and in the fear of God that I dare to address these questions. I know very well that we do not know how to talk about the Holy Spirit in a fitting manner. It seems almost sacrilegious to discuss this most sacred aspect of God as if it were a scientific object. It is alright to talk about God. Everyone has something of God in their hearts – some more, some less. The very being and character of God is evident in all people. The development of religions is a kind of proof of this aspect of human nature. This gives human intelligence the right to ask, "Who is God? Who is this God we should believe in?" God himself gives us, so to speak, his consent to use our own thinking to ask questions about him and to talk about him, even at the risk of being wrong. In the tangle of human opinions about God the true nature of God shines through again and again in many minds and hearts, like when the sun breaks through dark clouds. God lets upright men and women who are looking for truth gain an intuition that lifts them personally up to God, even if they know they are alone in this and find little fellowship. Something of God remains within the whole human race – indwelling, working, witnessing, and purifying them (cf. Rom. 1:19–20). This something of God can touch people who were born and raised in the jumble of false religions and gives them the right to talk about God according to their own view. And the Savior himself softens our judgment of those who utter falsehoods about God, saying that even blasphemy against God can be forgiven (Mark 3:28).

Christ was a man among men. The glory of God shone out from a man. His picture has been engraved into the hearts of millions of people, who sensed the reflection of these rays of glory in the Gospels. Their picture of Jesus remains as an inalienable gift of God, living among people. "The Word became flesh and made his dwelling among us" (John 1:14). Yes, and I might add that the Word *has been* dwelling among humankind throughout all centuries and *still* dwells among us to this very day – no matter what antagonistic opinions are spread about it. "What do you think of the Messiah?" (cf. Matt. 22:42) is a justified question, which may be laid before every thoughtful person and actually is being laid before them – even at the risk of someone blaspheming him. For judgment is also softened for someone who blasphemes the Son of God, the Son of Man. This sin is forgivable in the eyes of the Master of all godly affairs (Matt. 12:32a).

Our Relationship with the Holy Spirit

OUR RELATIONSHIP WITH the Holy Spirit is different. We shy away from talking about the Holy Spirit because wrong talk could bring disaster. For us human beings the Holy Spirit remains God's *holiest of all*: something which does not let itself be mixed with anything impure, something which we have no right to talk about unless we have experienced it, to the extent that it can be given to us under the circumstances. We can recognize the Spirit only when it imparts to us a specific message and even then, only insofar as the message actually reaches us. The Holy Spirit is sovereign. It withdraws from anyone it wishes and it reveals itself to anyone it wishes. It leads into the truth anyone it wishes and as far as it wishes, according to the holy will of the Creator of heaven and earth and all that lives therein (cf. John 3:8). Therefore, it is an unforgivable sin to blaspheme this spirit at the very moment when it wishes to make room in someone's heart for God's truth and his kingdom. It is a blasphemy against the truth itself, without which nobody can be a complete person, either in this world or the next. That is why it is also an unforgivable sin in this world and the next to slander and reject the Holy Spirit (Matt. 12:32b).

So, in general, I hesitate to talk about the Holy Spirit. All the more so because many people who do not discern the sacredness of the Holy Spirit are led into human misunderstanding because they think they can entertain thoughts about it as though it were simply subject to human understanding. We are wrong to think that the Holy Spirit automatically abides by human methods and customs. If that is what we believe, then we are merely thinking of the Spirit as a power that strengthens human convictions. People would like to think that any phenomenon with a Christian façade – even if it is bound to the most horrible superstition – must be a working of the Holy Spirit. Because of this view, by which all forms of Christianity lay claim to the Holy Spirit, it is obvious how carefully and with what reserve we have to talk about the Spirit. Otherwise we will be in danger of making the same mistake of desecrating something by making it serve our own interests, as opposed to serving the interests of God alone.

In spite of adverse opinions, I say most adamantly: the Holy Spirit must be given, and *is* given, only to magnify God and to transmit *his* life – not to reinforce contemporary human lifestyles or changing opinions. If you want to receive the Holy Spirit, if you are praying for the Holy Spirit, you should test your motives. Do you care about God and the revelation of his life, given in his eternal truth and righteousness? (Take note: his truth and righteousness combat any wrong, human developments.) Or do you desire the Spirit only for yourself, your own survival, and your personal salvation?

I pray that it may be given to me at this stage to give some notion of how elevated and sacred the Holy Spirit is. May it be given to me to admit it when I do not have this Holy Spirit, yet without becoming half-hearted in the hope of [actually] receiving the Spirit. We may receive the Spirit when our minds and hearts are purified enough to say no to all human desires, to sacrifice ourselves, and then to be on fire for God's creation so we can work for eternal truths and rights to permeate all of creation. As of now, our human ambiguities, which lead to the perversion of truth and justice, have obscured God's glory in his creation.

Creation and the Work of the Spirit

GOD SAID, "LET THERE BE LIGHT," and there was light (Gen. 1:3). That was the very beginning of the earth as we see it today, spread out before us with its manifold forms of life. It was an outpouring of the Holy Spirit over the chaos (Gen. 1:2). In this chaos elemental, embryonic life forms existed that gave promise for the development of higher life forms. But the outpouring of the Spirit eternally connects those life forms in their foundations with the Creator through their development, which occurs in every living thing according to its Creator's will. Humankind, as God's children – the first life form conscious of God and his spirit – has a responsibility in this life. Whoever can look away from himself and observe nature closely, with a pure mind, will be able to sense (in spite of all the confusion that has obscured on the exterior the actual nature of things) the Holy Spirit, which speaks eternally, but will not let itself be touched by unholy spirits (Rom. 1:19–20).

Anyone who is not on fire for God will not perceive him. Yet, in spite of all the opposition to truth in life (we call it sin), there remains a harmony between God and creation. This harmony originates in the Holy Spirit and even people who still feel excluded from this harmony can perceive it. They feel excluded because they are not at peace within themselves about their relationship to eternal things and because they know they have to die. For them death is bound to be a witness to the Holy One. Death permeates human society, where people set themselves at odds with creation because they have lost the Holy Spirit. The Holy One does not permit a life that is in opposition to his righteous life. A life full of contradictions dies of its own accord when it is faced with the eternal truths inherent in God's creation. It sinks back into primeval chaos, where it waits, lifeless, for a new revealing of God's spirit. But the Creator does not abandon what he has created: he does not leave it without hope, sunk in the death of its own making. Hope for resurrection soars up, the resurrection of Jesus, the true Son of God. The Holy Spirit, the spirit of creation, can turn creation's harmony with the Creator completely over to Jesus. In Jesus all created things can look forward to the new creation, redeemed from sin and death.

The Holy Spirit's Ongoing Work

HOWEVER, EVEN IN THE SON OF MAN the Holy Spirit remains ungraspable. No one can seize the Holy Spirit for himself; it must be given to us. The Holy Spirit does shine from now on, disclosing the Creator as the *Father of us all* in Jesus and glorifying him. [In the beginning] the light had to fight its way through the darkness to reach creation so that living things could come into being (to the extent that God willed) and give honor to their Creator. In the same way the new light of the new creation in Jesus – which will bring children of God into being – has to fight through the death residing in them. And just as all created beings had to go through a certain process of development before God said, "It is good," now, too, the new creation, which begins in the Son of Man, has to go through a process of development before we humans are completed, before we can say, "It is finished!"

We do not go through this transformation in our own strength, but only through the Holy Spirit. The Holy Spirit reveals itself by showing us the truths and laws of God. Our whole human nature has been in conflict with God's truth and justice until now. That's why we cannot truthfully say, "We are God's children." However, the Spirit (as revealed in Jesus) assures those who believe in Jesus that they are God's children (Romans 8:16), even though they are still a work in progress. What's more, the spirit of God's creation – the Holy Spirit, the spirit that dwelt in Jesus – is already at work in them and, even before their development reaches completion, brings about harmony between God and those people who are willing to get involved in this development. They can arrive at the point where the Holy Spirit lives in them and proceeds with their development until it is completed.

We can tell how little this spirit of God mingles with the spirit of humanity – how much it withdraws even from those who have received something of it – by the tremendous struggle each person has to take up against themselves and their flesh, and against the whole world and social order of their time (cf. Rom. 8:5–7; Gal. 5:17). If we look at the apostles and the prophets, we can see something like birth pangs. They wrestled for something they didn't have but for the sake of which they completely renounced their present lives. Though they may have found peace with God in the end, they suffered much unrest in the process. This unrest is the distinguishing mark of the Holy Spirit. If the pain should cease and peace return, this peace would soon show itself to be rotten, just as with a woman when the birth pangs cease and the child dies before it is born.

The Holy Spirit's Work Completed

OBVIOUSLY, THEREFORE, there is no point in looking for the Holy Spirit where people are satisfied with the present, permeated as it is with sin and death; where people have gotten used to living with lies (lies they are fully aware of). Where – I might as well say it bluntly – there is no revolution clearing the way for something new and more perfect. Another obvious conclusion is that people who have received the Holy Spirit in some measure and who feel connected to the Creator as their Father through Jesus Christ will seek and wait almost fearfully for the Holy Spirit, because they want to make progress in the Spirit and in truth, lest they fall from the tree of life like rotten fruit (Matt. 7:17, 12:33; Luke 6:43–45). They realize that though God gives the Spirit without limit (John 3:34), he does not give his spirit into vessels that are already three quarters full with another spirit, leaving only a small space. They know that if some measure of the spirit of God has touched and shaken them, now it is their responsibility to make every effort to clear out their entire being so that God's holiness can fill them *completely.* And they are worried that the measure of the Spirit they have received will depart if they do not make every effort to give it sole authority over them no matter what. For the Holy Spirit will not house with an unclean spirit unless the person unites in spirit with the Holy Spirit (Rom. 8:16), so that the sharp sword of the Holy Spirit can fight within them against all remaining selfishness, even in their body (cf. Heb. 4:12). Then at least progress is being made toward complete surrender and God is given his due, even though much has yet to be overcome. In light of the above, we see the right reasons that moved my father to pray for a new outpouring of the Holy Spirit. But we will also see why his request could not yet be fully granted to the extent he wished.

The Promise of Direct Guidance

MY FATHER SAW QUITE RIGHTLY that the Holy Spirit, viewed from our perspective, is the part of God that God keeps secluded. The Holy Spirit draws near to us only occasionally, when it reveals God and his will. Then it stays with us, living within us as the spirit of sonship and peace of God, only as long as we use the revelation given to us to benefit God's kingdom. Closely connected to this is the realization that we can always look forward to the Holy Spirit giving us something new, something that will glorify God until the consummation of all things in perfect truth. Because my father strove for the coming of God's kingdom, he felt instinctively that there needed to be continuous forward movement – always something new – for God's cause to advance. He found this idea to be fully confirmed by the stories of men of God in the Bible.

In Abraham we can already see a man whom God's spirit moved to a stage of life in which he could become the father of a nation that testi- fies to the living God (Gen. 12:2, 17:4). That was not the end of striving for more gifts. God's spirit came near again, to Moses, bringing a completely new stage under new circumstances. This time the whole nation was given God's laws, so that they would be able to witness to God by obeying the laws revealed to them. And again, new light came with new revelations – this time more obviously given through the Holy Spirit – during the time of David and the prophets, who were solidly founded on this new revelation. At this stage it clearly becomes justifiable to expect new revelations. From this stage on, the expression "outpouring of the Holy Spirit" is in general use (Joel 2:28–29; Ezek. 11:19, 36:26–27). Seeing beyond their own times and circumstances, the prophets spoke (in their zeal for the knowledge of God) about a renewal of the people through the Holy Spirit. In this renewal, the

Holy Spirit will change hearts and create a true people of God, to whom God can be fully God (cf. Jer. 31:27–34). Besides this, the prophets speak of an outpouring of the Holy Spirit over all people (Joel 2:28) and see the future of God's kingdom as belonging to all nations (Acts 2:17–18). God's Word, which was brought to Abraham as a seed by God's spirit, has already grown into a tree for the prophets – a tree with the promise of wonderful fruit.

This wonderful fruit became visible in Jesus, the Son of Man, and his disciples. The direct presence of God, the Holy Spirit, came upon a small flock (Luke 12:32) and created new people, thereby establishing a new people of God that was no longer held in check by laws. Instead, under the rule of freedom, this people, born of one spirit, pursued one goal and was led by God himself. When this wonderful fruit became visible, it was the beginning of the fulfillment of prophecy, but not yet the completion.

Precisely at this stage, the people of God are more dependent on *constant revelations of God* than at earlier stages, because all making of statutes falls away on principal and the free rule of God begins in the heart. The apostles could not imagine their ministry without constant new revelations or without continuous new outpouring of the Holy Spirit – without that they could not even share with strangers the grace of God they had received, not even with a powerful, convincing sermon. The Holy Spirit had to be poured out in Samaria, in Caesarea, in Philippi, in Corinth, and everywhere (Acts 4:31, 8:15–17, 10:44–47, 19:6; 1 Cor. 1:5–7) so that God himself could give the full measure of grace to those who were called, the full measure as given to the apostles for their time and their world.

If the outpouring of the Holy Spirit ceased, believers started instituting new laws. And then they lost faith and did not dare to advance in freedom any further through being taught by God himself. This is exactly what threw the apostle Paul into his battles against reinstituting Judaic Laws in Christian circles. They wanted to re-impose laws as a substitute for what God had planned to accomplish through the Holy Spirit alone (cf. Gal. 3:1–5). The radical position that Paul took against imposing laws or statutes justifies for all time our need to pray for a new outpouring of the Holy Spirit. Either we have to abandon Paul's position – he depended solely on revelation – or we have to depend on revelation too. However, there is now no other revelation than the one brought by Jesus Christ and exercised through the gifts of the Holy Spirit. Neither the letter of the scriptures nor a sermon imbued with faith can bring about what has to be accomplished in human hearts on the foundation of Jesus Christ to the glory of God.

When the Spirit Is Absent

BUT IN THE PRESSURES of difficult times, Christianity departed from relying on the direct guidance of God. Instead Christians tried to advance Christ's lordship in their human zeal, and that is why the church has turned into an institution propped up by laws. The church wanted to build God's kingdom with the same measures that secular rulers use to build and fortify worldly kingdoms. But in this way the church betrayed the essential nature of the new life that had come through Jesus Christ. Even though Christ himself could not be totally eliminated as the mediator of God's grace in revelations of the Holy Spirit, church ordinances had much more influence on the hearts of men and women than the authority of God. Essentially human laws ruled, and in the course of time they have produced a Christendom in accordance with the laws that human society makes to suit its own development.

Christians tried by legislation to establish a catholic church – a fellowship spread throughout the world. The attempt failed. But for centuries Christians have pursued this goal so tenaciously and persistently that we suffer from it to this very day. In Protestant circles, too, Christians think that the power of faith is closely connected to laws, and that is why many think God's people are protected mainly by the laws and only incidentally by the Holy Spirit. On the other hand, it is a great grace that the Protestant churches cannot find unity based on their rules of faith and church laws. Through the Reformation, enough of God's will is alive in Protestant churches that we at least, in spite of strenuous efforts, have not been able to come to unity based on church laws. In the back of our minds, we hear Christ saying, "I have trodden the winepress alone" (Isa. 63:3), and that he will rule (cf. 1 Cor. 15:25) until he has a people who will no longer fall for the illusion that all we need is certain religious systems and that is the end of the matter; until he has a people who depend on God's revelation alone; and until a new outpouring of the Holy Spirit – over many or just a few – will prove that this is the one and only way that God can bring his kingdom to earth and perfect it.

Come Holy Spirit!

TO HOPE FOR A NEW OUTPOURING of the Holy Spirit is consistent with what my father experienced when he called out into the world, "Jesus is victor!" Jesus is certainly *not* victor if new legislation or new church ordinances are supposed to gain the victory. In that case human beings are the victors, and God's perfect will and his righteousness in all truth cannot come into their own. Even our faith tends to take its cues not so much from Christ as from the human laws we are used to and that have been drilled into us. However, I declare emphatically that with human laws we will *never* get to the bottom of things. We would not even be able to eradicate the worst superstitions, let alone everything else that our human selfishness brings with it. Truth has to come out of your heart, not from people or through people, but from God in the name of Jesus Christ through the outpouring of the Holy Spirit.

Anyone can see these things who does not place himself and his own happiness in first place, but who, instead, at the cost of his happiness, offers himself as a living sacrifice to God (Rom. 12:1) so that God will gain his rightful claim on earth.

Of course, anyone who does not understand the battle that Jesus leads us into will not even want to know anything about a new outpouring of the Holy Spirit. The battle means we have to sacrifice ourselves at the cross and honor God and not be satisfied until God alone is glorified. God's people are now facing a time when they are called into battle against their own flesh, not for their own sakes or for their own eternal salvation, but so that they can be made into vessels for God, vessels in which God's Holy One can live powerfully and victoriously and from which he can go out into the world. Those who do not understand this will not be interested in a new outpouring of the Holy Spirit. They make do with the assurance that whatever faith was injected into them, depending on their religious upbringing, will be enough to save them through God's mercy. At most such people might attempt to draw *other people* into *their* church so they can also happily say, "Now we are saved!" Such people have no concept of the great calling in Christ. If they did, they would realize that such a calling is not attained through Christian education or by adapting to current Christian rules, but only through the outpouring of the Holy Spirit. We have to believe in the Holy Spirit – our confessions of faith call for it. The only way to express this belief is to realize that we have to stand ready to receive new revelations of God's will. His will continuously unfolds for his people, revealing everything that is needed for different times until God's kingdom comes in its fullness.

On the basis of this belief, I am convinced that it was my father's good fortune (and ours as well) that in spite of being rejected on every side, he never stopped directing his life according to this hope. He accomplished more for the kingdom of God in this way than in any other way, even when he was only praying quietly to God. If he would have given in on *this* point – if he had relinquished his hope for the sake of people who felt satisfied with what Christianity is able to accomplish through academics and the arts, through enthusiasm and hard work – then his spiritual lampstand in heaven might have been totally removed (Rev. 2:5). Then we would hardly have any right to base our existence on his experiences. It was crucial for us to honor the Holy Spirit, and it is still crucial today. We have to glorify it by separating it from anything impure. We will not attribute to the Holy Spirit a movement that may be three quarters due to human good will and common sense or to sincere Christian zeal for the scriptures, while only one quarter is inspired by the Holy Spirit. We must honor the Holy Spirit as something much holier, something that can sweep through our life bringing truth and justice. We must never give up hoping that it is possible for this Most Holy One to come from God to earth. Yes, he most certainly will come – when the time is fulfilled when God, according to his plan, will separate the just from the unjust, the true from the false, the eternal from the perishable.

Preparing for the Holy One

WE COULD, OF COURSE, make do with less. Like my father, we could simply entrust to God's will how, when, and where the Holy Spirit will appear again. But I cannot quite put my mind at ease like that. The scriptures have convinced me that people who are called to God's kingdom are also called to *work for him*. We see in scripture that everything God has done to benefit his kingdom on earth has bonded only with people who were willing to be pruned. This is a solid principle in the kingdom of God, with no exceptions. Even the birth of Jesus was not given without Simeon, a repentant man, whose longing was a rebuke to his time and his people. Similarly, a prerequisite for the outpouring of the Holy Spirit during apostolic times was a group of people who had allowed themselves to be prepared as pure vessels for the Holy Spirit.

Now we can see that to hope and pray for the Holy Spirit, the giver of all holy gifts, is a serious matter. In effect we have to look away from God's spirit and turn against ourselves by asking, "Who are we to be asking for the Holy Spirit? Can this Holy Spirit – as we have come to know it through the scriptures – be given into unclean, unworthy vessels?" As long as we cling to any remnant of our selfish nature – either intentionally, as to customary traditions, or even unintentionally – we will pray in vain for the Holy Spirit.

This is the same as saying to God, "We are pleased with your spirit, but there are certain things we won't relinquish for it because we are so used to them."

To pray means going to work on ourselves. You can ask God for whatever you like, but you cannot escape the question, "Am I fit to receive what I am asking for?" Through Jesus Christ there should be enough of God's power in the world by this time that those who believe in Jesus can look at their own lives and judge for themselves. They should know enough about the kingdom of God (which is entirely different from a worldly kingdom) to see that they will have to deny themselves and sacrifice everything in order to gain what God wants to give. This is and always will be the requirement that God has every right to place on us.

No matter what it is you are looking forward to, you will not receive it without accepting the blood of Jesus Christ, without your sinful nature dying in his death. There is no other way for us to receive anything. You may experience a gradual change – for example, you may receive all kinds of blessings, to the extent that you deny yourself and sacrifice yourself to a certain degree in the blood of Jesus. It may be that you receive all kinds of help in troubles and afflictions through Jesus Christ the victor, as you submit to him and honor his authority. But in respect to receiving the Holy Spirit itself, I have been shown that we must be willing to *sacrifice* our entire being to the core, with all we have and are; we must die with Christ and diminish ourselves, so that this holy being – the Most Holy One – will not consume us with holy fire but, instead, will grant us life through Jesus Christ's resurrection. Our spirit must yield. Even anything relatively good that we may have achieved has to fall away. Our human character, even if it looks respectable in comparison to other characters, has to surrender in order to make room for the Holy Spirit.

"God gives the Spirit without limit." It is not enough for you to open only part of your heart for the Holy Spirit – to let him lead you only partway – and meanwhile reserve the rest for yourself, maybe even the biggest share! No, you must free up your whole heart for God, so that the Spirit can fill you completely. It should not be obliged to live in you next to anything impure, ungodly, sinful, or malignant. The time will come, and may already be here, when the Savior will refuse to tolerate any other company, any other spirits that want to influence us. It is the same with our own flesh – he wants to know that we have cast it out before he will send the Holy Spirit to us without limit. If we set no limits, he will fully refine us and make us holy.

Unless we pass this strict judgment on ourselves, we can pray and beg as much as we like, but nothing will change. Even anything we do in the name of Jesus will be no different or hardly different from what other people do in the name of truth, justice, or love to humankind.

So now maybe you can understand why we still take the same position today, even though my father did not live to see the fulfillment of his prayer for the Holy Spirit. With body and soul we uphold the Holy Spirit as the greatest hope for the world. But as we approach this highest and greatest gift of God, which will one day bless all creation, we want to *put ourselves under judgment* and not cling to anything that comes from below, anything from this world (John 8:23). We will not intermingle this spirit with anything or anyone worldly, no matter what a big name or reputation someone may have.

15

Hope for a Zion

WHAT MY FATHER EXPERIENCED in Möttlingen became a mighty foundation stone, on which his hopes were built. He had seen the congregation at Möttlingen recreated. Three observations made a lasting impression on him, as he thought about what had happened to this bunch of people. First of all, to his surprise and without any conscious effort on his part, a completely new time broke out for these people. All of a sudden there was a difference in the way people thought, felt, and lived their daily lives. The new meaning that now pervaded all of life radiated quite naturally from the thought, "God is truly among us, in Jesus, the victor over all the powers of sin and death coming from the abyss."

My father's second remarkable observation was that the new time for these people (to their surprise and without any conscious effort on their part) influenced others in the world around them. Spiritual threads spread out in all directions, so that without any human zeal or drive for results this new time attracted all kinds of people from near and far.

Finally, the third distinguishing feature of this new time was that the differences between people no longer mattered or seemed to evaporate. This held true with uncompromising power. Anything of historical or human significance that clings to a person like a vine could no longer be counted as part of that individual. Social differences were unimportant; so were religious differences. In the new time we were appalled if anyone judged a person by whether he was born upper class or lower class, Catholic or Protestant. All that mattered was the individual, stripped of the past. No covering, either inner or outer, made any difference. The new time led people directly to *eternal* things, to the working of God – and to our surprise God's working turned out to be nonpartisan and world encompassing.[1]

The New amid the Old

MY FATHER DID NOT SEPARATE his experience of eternal things from the old time in which he lived quite as clearly as I have just done. Although his spirit jubilated in his experience of the eternal, he remained loyal in a small degree to the life of the flesh as manifested in human practices and especially historically rooted traditions. So what happened is that through his experience, a mighty hope for a new time for all humankind took root in him and grew into a strong living plant that could not be uprooted anymore. But, at the same time, with this great hope some selfish hopes were included. Some of his wishes and prayers sprang more from his compassion for unfortunate people than from his sympathy for God and his kingdom. My father's hope for a new time welled up out of his heart. Even when he was near death he still gave us this legacy: "The Lord will open his mild hand in mercy over all nations."[2] This made it very clear which direction our hope should move. But a loophole was left open for many (who were swept along by this hope) to combine it with desires of the flesh and a false chiliasm, or striving for a Christian millennium, which from of old has spoiled the hopes of Christians.[3] In this way, God's eternity was [measured by and] reduced to human constructs of time. As I have mentioned several times already, even my father was susceptible to making the same mistake, since along with his efforts to seek God and his kingdom and to proclaim Christ as the sole victor, he wasted some of his zeal defending Christian practices of his day. Basically, he sacrificed too much time and energy on human interests.

At least he did not fall for the other mistake of letting a faction or sect gather around his person or even forming one himself. He was too strongly impressed by the eternal powers at work in the new time, which far exceeded any human desires, for that to happen. He had so clearly seen God's supreme power working freely – free of any human methods or [charismatic] personalities – that he was worlds away from making that mistake. His decision to leave the congregation at Möttlingen proves this. He felt

---

1 Compare Zündel, 512–519.

2 See Zundel, 524.

3 For the difference between the elder Blumhardt's hopes and chiliastic strivings, see Sauter, *Die Theologie des Reiches Gottes*, 56ff.; Johann Christoph Blumhardt, *Ausgewählte Werke*, vol. 1, 134f.

that *God's Zion* did not depend on any place or any group of people. God creates his temple on earth, built of living stones (1 Pet. 2:5; 1 Cor. 3:16–17), by himself. No human hand can add anything or take away anything. God's temple comes down to earth and takes effect wherever and however he alone decides.

Longing for Zion

WHEN I INTRODUCED this theme I called it my father's "hope for Zion." With this term I am closely uniting with the hopes that shine brightly throughout the history of Abraham's people, in which the Spirit was poured out on men of God. Ultimately all these hopes group around the concept of "Zion." I like this expression because "Zion" is not used for a physical *place*, a place that can be corrupted by people, like the city of Jerusalem is – even though its earthly name does come from the palace of David.[4] If we take a look at how these spiritual men of Israel lived, from Abraham down to the apostles, what they fought for and spoke up for, then we can say: they lived in Zion, they cared for Zion, and they upheld the Zion of God. It is the life that comes from God which becomes the eternal homeland for people *on earth*. It is the life of God *on earth* that makes humanity human and enables them to further develop into the image of God. It is the revelation of God *on earth* that is needed, otherwise the salvation of the nations is not possible. When taken together, all the human witnesses to God in the Bible – among whom Jesus Christ stands as the focal point – tell us that God, who became one with humanity, wants to live *on earth*, bringing forth from himself in a constant overflow everything that is needed for the life of creation. Insofar as that which is pure, true, and eternal from God can dwell on earth, what we call Zion will grow up around those people who watch for it.

In this way Abraham already lived in Zion. Out of Zion came the promises given to him that proclaimed salvation. Out of Zion came the blessings that surrounded him. Moses was accepted into Zion and led the people, as directed by the Spirit, not into the wilderness, but into God's Zion, where the people could see justice and truth and feel life at work doing things that were incomprehensible to other people. And later whenever people were accepted into this domain of God, their hearts and mouths were open for God and his eternal truth, and something of God's reign, his justice, and his

---

4 In the Bible, "Zion" was initially used for geographic places: the city of David, then the Temple Mount, and later the quarter where the early church lived. Aside from that, already in biblical times, "Zion" was used for the promise of God's church in the end times. This is the sense in which Christoph Blumhardt uses it.

kingdom was visible in the world. In this Zion the prophets could embrace the world. Forgetting themselves, they saw the salvation of the nations. In this Zion they could see anything unholy vanish before what was holy. For them, the light of Zion turned into a fire that consumed anything impure so that only what was pure would touch the life of Zion.

Jesus was born into this domain of God. He was the firstborn Son of God as none other before him. He served God with body and soul. With both his inner and outer being he served God, who permeates heaven and earth as Father. That is why Jesus could say: "I and the Father are one" (John 10:30). The only way we can understand the signs that happened around him, which he called "the works of his Father" (cf. John 9:4, 10:25, 14:10) is by realizing that they came out of this Zion. It was on this divine basis that Jesus could bring the sinful world to God through his blood. His resurrection made him the permanent center of God's Zion on earth. Through this anyone who is willing to abandon his or her flesh and die to the flesh for the sake of the work of God on earth can gain entrance into Zion – or into heaven, as it is now called. For this is what the heavenly kingdom of Jesus Christ is; it is whatever God creates *on earth* in order to prepare a dwelling place for people that is outside the realm of sin and death. These are also the "rooms" of the Father in heaven (John 14:2), which Jesus will prepare since he is the one resurrected from the dead. For as *the resurrected one* he belongs to *the earth* and has a physical claim on the earth. Therefore, he can prepare heavenly dwellings, or dwellings that belong to the Father, here on earth. No longer shall human beings be the only ones to work and produce on earth, but God will work with them, and his working will undermine and overturn any false human work. For justice and righteousness will go out from Zion (Isa. 2:3), and the reign of God will come from this place of his on earth.

God's Zion and the Church

THIS IS HOW WE FEEL and what we hope for today. Not in uncertainty, as my father did. We hope for a "new time," as if we would suddenly wake up on a beautiful morning and see Mount Zion outside our window, as if in some incomprehensible way a new time of jubilation and triumph would open up for us. Strictly speaking, we do not need a new time in the sense that many people imagine such a new time – that is, when people will enjoy better living conditions and it will be easier to gain eternal salvation. What we need, rather, is for eternal powers to come work for God and his reign, so that the wrong dominion of the human spirit comes to an end and God's pure reign takes over. In the wake of human rule, we see only bleeding corpses. For human rule, millions of lives are slaughtered. Only when God governs will life really become life, and God's creation will be able to rise from the disgrace of the flesh.

You can see, from what I have written so far, how this hope for Zion expels us from much of so-called Christian thought. To start with, the fame of the Christian church fades before our eyes. It should never have claimed to be the Zion of God, the exclusive place and the sole spiritual entity through which we can approach God. The glory of any human greatness fades, where people want to force others to accept a certain spiritual orientation. Before our eyes so-called historic institutions fade – whether contained in books or buildings or traditions – for the Most High does not live in temples made by human hands (Acts 7:48–50; cf. 2 Sam. 7:6; 1 Kings 8:27). We see clearly into the past, the present, and what is coming. As a people of Zion, we do not want to be stuck in the past or hanker for the good old days. Because we are hoping for Zion, we see the present as only a station, which we will leave behind when the time comes. We guard against thinking complete fulfillment was given either in the past or in the present.

Because we are waiting for Zion, we are well aware that we need to change. We cannot rest in the present. Instead we are quite prepared for any change, even if it leads to the breakup of what we hold dear. As our example we do not take Christianity, or a church, or a confession, or the life of a saint, but only the Zion of God with its perfect forms of life. Of course, as of now we can only see these perfect forms in general outline, not yet in detail. But through the Spirit of Zion, we have recognized enough that we are in dead earnest when we dare to say in words similar to Paul's, "We will forget what is behind and what is in the present, and we will strain toward what lies ahead" (Phil. 3:13). We will most certainly share in past and present eternal powers of God, too, if we keep our eyes on the future, while staying flexible with the fear of God in our hearts. This future will be *on earth*, to the glory of the great Creator and the Master among the nations.

Many people may not be able to understand how we can go on, lightheartedly, without crusading for anything or anybody in our turbulent time. We know that everything is in good hands. Things which are meant to break will break; things riddled with death will die. When the rafters built up by the flesh tumble down, the eternal power of God will be kept safe without any human assistance. God's eternal power does not judge according to a person's reputation and does not minister to the selfish clamor of peoples and nations or the outcry of generations and societies for the desires of their flesh. But we also do not need to help overturn anything that does not seem right to us. Woe to us if we should want to be revolutionaries with our human hands, or if we should want to build up Zion with our human hands. But when the Spirit of Zion breaks free and joins the freedom which is in Christ, when the Spirit of Zion liberates us from the false love of our flesh and the fleshly desires of humanity, then who will hinder it? We know that Zion is coming from heaven and is already working. We can rest assured and wait for what that time will bring that is united with eternity – when God's will, and not humankind's will, shall be done on earth as it is in heaven.

The Presence of God's Future

THIS HOPE FOR ZION changes our spiritual direction still further. Sitting in the central core of Christian thought there is a worm, which we also fed in earlier days. It is the worm that has taught people to think that God is not interested in this world and that people should only be concerned with heaven. Even people of noble character say publicly that Christ has nothing to do with shaping human conditions on earth. They say Christ directs us to think only about the invisible world. I do not want to have anything to do with this worm anymore because the *opposite* is true: Christ became *flesh*, so as to destroy the world of the flesh and establish the work of God *on earth*. Truth and justice have already been valid for a long time in God's domains and for his other creations. They shall become a visible part of the earth and its inhabitants too. This is Christ, and there is no other. Christ died for this, and for this God raised him up and promised him the future on earth. Anyone who invents another Christ beats the true Christ to death and makes him a laughing stock. It is a crying shame that people are not willing to be set on fire by this Christ who brings the kingdom of God to earth – so set on fire that they truly seek on earth what God wanted to give through Christ.

But of course God does not exist according to our conceited wishes. He does not exist in our untruthfulness. He does not exist for our desire for money and power. He exists for the benefit of the truth, for the benefit of life, and for the judgment of the flesh and the destruction of sin. People have done a mighty fine job of imagining a different heaven for themselves, a heaven where Christ is a "good enough" guarantee, which lets them continue fooling around in their casual pursuits. Of course, God's heaven is not like that! As God's Zion, it sheds light on the earth. In the face of this heaven, O flesh, you will shake. O injustice and untruth, you will quake! No form of human authority counts here, nor any pretense of self-made holiness. All that counts is the inexorable thread of justice and truth.

If the seriousness of Zion captures our soul, then good for us! If through Christ we become such worshipers of God that our first concern is for God to reign, then good for us! Then the salvation of the nations will be possible. Who among today's Christians really expects to see the salvation of the nations? Who expects to see the final good of the nations to come from our churches and temples, from any human holiness or contemporary church services? Who wants to bless the world with the present, call it what you like? Anyone who sincerely considers God would not do that, for even the best is still poisoned. We are still walking in the mire and are unable to rid our lives of the vines of lies and greed. But in Zion we see victory over the dragon of this flesh, who spits his poison into everything, so that even the noblest conceptions of God have to draw back in order to avoid the spittle of the false, godless spirits of this flesh.

Who can hold it against me if I say that striving for bliss and salvation after death is a disastrous worm in the Christian life? This truth speaks for itself, and I do not want to waste a single word in its defense. I am certainly not saying, "Fear death, for then you will be hopelessly lost!" The opposite is true: God cares for his own and for all people in both this world and the next. That is exactly why everyone should not get stuck spending all their energies on getting saved after death. In almost no Christian era could fighters for God's kingdom come to the fore because of all the fear about personal salvation. This striving for bliss is a hidden poison that distorts our love for God. Almost without exception it fills the hearts of pious people, both Christian and heathen alike. But if we really love God, that is very different from loving ourselves. To be Israel, God's fighter, is very different from winning a life of bliss after death.

What do we thank the prophets for today? Not that they were saved themselves, but that they struggled to portray for this earth a clear picture of God, the God who belongs to the earth as its creator. We thank them that they risked their own lives and the lives of their people to prepare the way for the appearance of the anointed one, so that the Christ could come, in whom God establishes his authority on earth. For this they called out, "Build up, build up, prepare the road! Remove the obstacles out of the way of my people!" (Isa. 57:14). For this they cried, "Arise, shine, for your light has come, and the glory of the Lord rises upon you. . . . Nations will come to your light!" (Isa. 60:1, 3). We thank God for what was made possible on earth through the apostles and prophets, for the light of Jesus that was on earth and still is. We, too, want to give our last drop of blood to benefit this cause. We want to sacrifice ourselves so that this earth will be won over for God.

The Struggle for Zion

THE BATTLE IS NOT OVER yet. Sin has deceived us and put a false Christ on the throne. We hoodwink ourselves by looking for a righteousness that will give us salvation and let everything else continue to go to the dogs. Truly, in light of this paralyzing poison in our members, I think the way the world strives for progress is quite admirable. This striving at least demonstrates an honest recognition that we are not what we should be and do not have what it takes to be people of truth. However, what is gained by all the striving and wrestling of the forsaken nations? What is gained through the sacrificed blood of their soldiers? At most a temporary rise of a nation or world empire; but no sooner does it rise than already a chasm opens up and the elevated nation falls. Therefore, a different striving must be introduced into this striving of the nations, which works without hate or any desire to condemn – which works in the love that overcomes death. This striving comes to help the nations struggling in the throes of death. Through God's power, this striving is able to open up those paths on which the very foundation of our human existence is changed and purified. Then it develops into a foundation, which of its own accord expels anything unjust or untrue. I call such striving a striving for Zion. It is not an unfruitful hope that inspires us to hope for Zion. Rather, we enter with our whole being into a battle on earth against anything of the flesh, first and foremost in ourselves. Our hope demands it.

So we go to work with hope. And what is this work? We certainly do not presume to convert other people or to criticize those who do not and cannot think the way we do. Those who have any inkling of Zion will be ashamed of themselves first of all, for they know that the hardest battle they have to fight is within their own hearts. Their own flesh has built up a stronghold that needs to be conquered. Those who are hoping for God's Zion to come on earth will seek to order their own affairs and to put themselves under God's judgment, in order to destroy whatever belongs to death and let whatever God creates arise as a new person.

But how does this work benefit *the nations*? What does this struggle achieve for *the whole earth* – when just a few individuals are willing to die to themselves for the sake of God and for Zion? It is not our responsibility to figure this out. All we know is that threads have gone out into the whole world from the cross of Jesus Christ, the bearer of sin. Therefore, he is now called Lord over everything that is in heaven and on earth (Matt. 28:18; Phil. 2:9–11) and in him the end of all flesh has been announced. Alone and forsaken, he dies on the cross for his Father in heaven. He does not consider his own life because he loves his Father. He gives himself unto death, since our body of flesh cannot enter the kingdom of God. He has conquered death as the solitary one. In him, the head, his body will also win, not through human struggles by human powers against human authorities, but through his self-sacrifice of his own blood. If we die in Christ we shall also reign with him (2 Tim. 2:11). Such a people, willing to die, will receive authority from God. From this small flock, in which Jesus can live, threads will go out throughout the whole earth. Such dying prepares the way for resurrection and the victory of the kingdom of God, which gives true life and true forms of life.

This, dear friends, is our *hope for Zion*. Please forgive me if I have said too much. Please think about it quietly and remember: whatever is true remains true. Truth does not need to be justified. It will make room for itself, for it is of God, the Almighty.

16

Death Will Be Swallowed Up

THERE IS ANOTHER HOPE, which follows directly as a necessary sequel to the hope for a Zion. It is almost more unbelievable than anything we have discussed so far. I would rather not speak about it, just as I am writing all of these essays with much trepidation. For not only the expectation of the Holy Spirit and the establishment of God's kingdom and God's authority in a Zion, but even more so the ensuing hope of resurrection are so far removed from all previous experience in the development of the nations that it seems presumptuous to try to live by something so different from what the rest of the world is living through. Yet the hope for resurrection is part and parcel of seeking for the kingdom of God, and the abolition of death itself is an undeniable part of God's kingdom. Those who do not have the courage to consider this seriously or to get personally involved in the battle against death (when the time draws near in which death will be brought to light as the last *enemy*, as Paul calls it [1 Cor. 15:26]) cannot be called disciples of Jesus.

What about Death?

WE ONLY NEED TO REMEMBER the resurrection of Jesus Christ, and the question comes up: What is it about death, which so powerfully controls us and the whole human race? The apostle Paul saw himself directly confronted with this question. For this reason he argued with the Corinthians, who said there was no resurrection of the dead, even though they believed in the resurrection of Christ. He told them straight to their faces: "If there is no resurrection of the dead (that is, if the abolition of death for humanity is not possible), then not even Christ has been raised. And if Christ has not been raised, our preaching is useless and so is your faith. For as in Adam *all* die, so in Christ *all* will be made alive. . . . For he must reign until he has put all his enemies under his (the Father's) feet. The last enemy to be destroyed is death. . . . I declare to you, brothers and sisters, that flesh and blood (in which death rules) cannot inherit the kingdom of God, nor does the perishable inherit the imperishable. Listen, I tell you a mystery: We will not all sleep, but we will all be changed" (1 Cor. 15:12–51). The apostle Paul fixed his attention squarely on the goal, and he must be right if there is anything at all to Christ as he has been testified to for us. For the glory of God as revealed on earth in the person of Jesus was not only grace and truth but also resurrection and life. "I am the resurrection and the life" bursts from his lips. "The one who believes in me will not die, and whoever lives by believing in me will never die" (John 11:25–26).

The Abolition of Death

IN CHRIST, AS TESTIMONY to him bears witness, all God's words and all his works breathe of the *abolition of death*. What is the eternal life of which John said: "That which was from the beginning, which we have heard, which we have seen with our eyes, which we have looked at and our hands have touched – this we proclaim concerning the Word of life. The life appeared; we have seen it and testify to it, and we proclaim to you the eternal life, which was with the Father and has appeared to us" (1 John 1:1–2)? What was it that they all saw? For example, when the disciples of John the Baptist asked Jesus: "Where do you live?" and they were invited with these words: "Come and *see*" – "they went and *saw*" and afterwards they said: "We have found the one Moses wrote about in the Law and about whom the prophets also wrote" (John 1:38–39, 45). What did they see? Did they see a hut? Or a palace? Or a scholarly man? Or a strong character? We get an indication of what they saw by the words of Jesus at the end of this story: "Very truly I tell you, you will see heaven open, and the angels of God ascending and descending on the Son of Man" (John 1:51). The eternal life of the kingdom of God appeared to them in the flesh. The eternal life of the kingdom, which though still with the Father [in its perfection], had asserted itself in and through Jesus as a harbinger of the abolition of death. The disciples began to understand and be sensitive to this eternal life, even though they still had to struggle a lot, and even though they themselves, sad to say, fell again into darkness and unbelief, so that Jesus rebuked them for their lack of faith after his resurrection (Mark 16:14). Nevertheless, they saw death as a power that had been overcome in and around Jesus. And later on the apostles led the churches to the point where even though their members still died, the believers could see the light of life shining so brightly already that the resurrection of the dead became a reality and a transformation of those who were still living so that they could live their physical life as if death were no longer powerful.[1]

Of course, the first concern of those who had spiritually died with Jesus and risen with him was not yet the impending battle with death. Whereas their life was hid with Christ in God and they were personally at peace – beyond the power of death – they still had to endure sorrow, fear, need, and death in this physical life. Nevertheless, the prime goal of all their labors was to defeat the last enemy. Only when death is overcome will the kingdom of God be visible on earth for all nations to see. But for the present, they had to conquer other enemies of God's kingdom that came to the fore. They knew that Christ was seated in heaven, whence he could destroy all authorities, powers, and spiritual forces that are not of God the Father. And they knew he was with them, the members of his body on earth, so that they could consciously take part in this battle against all powers and authorities of darkness (Eph. 6:12) and against all power of the flesh.

So we see the apostles initially engaged in *these* battles, and their words and testimonies about the kingdom of God in Christ – which have come down to us in the form of exhortations to the churches – are mainly a fruit of these battles against the enemies that were close at hand. It was not the right time to tackle death itself as long as there was so much superstition, idolatry, and the related demonic suppression of spirits, and as long as people, even if they had accepted Christ, were still in great danger of being overcome by the human spirit (the flesh) that surrounded them on all sides. Instead they had to clear a path in the visible world as well as in the invisible world for the gospel of the kingdom – in Christ, the crucified and risen one. All spirits and spiritual forces in heaven and on earth resisted the kingdom of God, and so the believers had to summon up all their faith and totally deny themselves through the Holy Spirit, if only to open the way for the proclamation of life. This is why the abolition of death as the last power was mentioned only occasionally. It was kept as a secret, but a secret with which all true witnesses of God in Christ are familiar. In the days of the apostles there were so many possible battles in this world of unbelief and so many enemies that the clear light the warriors of God were fighting for – God's kingdom, God's justice, and God's life – was obscured by dark clouds.

---

1 Allusions to this in 1 Thess. 4:13–18; 1 Cor. 11:30, 15:54–55.

Our Approach to Death

IT HAS NOT BEEN GRANTED to us to see the details, but this much is obvious today: this conviction of the resurrection of all life, which was the basic premise for everything the apostles of Jesus Christ and the early churches talked about and did, was later abandoned. After Jerusalem was destroyed [in AD 70], the apostles' testimony falls silent; we do not know whether they were still living or not. It was then that the believers' burning expectation for the great goal of God's kingdom began to cool. This apathy spread so far that, from that time on, the only fire or fervor we can detect is on behalf of the church. The church no longer regarded death as an enemy but rather as a friend. The church also no longer regarded the flesh in the form of human power and authority as an *enemy* but as a *friend*. Christians no longer longed to experience the kingdom of God on earth, but instead worked zealously to develop a Christian religion and thereby gain worldly power in order to compete with heathen religions. In the process, the goals God had revealed through the Holy Spirit were forgotten. Instead everyone rejoiced when they realized that the Christian religion now had the conquering sword of the world on its side.

In the same way, this enemy – death – also sneaked into the inner circles of believers as a friend. The inner circles, as a quiet and peaceful people of Zion, should have been fighting against death at all times with the weapon of eternal life. In the beginning it may well have been in a good sense that believers welcomed death as a deliverer from all pain in the midst of persecution and temporal distress, but gradually this turned into disastrous stupidity. They did not realize how this posture more and more exiled the essential truth of Christ – the fact that he is risen from the dead. As though they were partially stupefied, the believers transformed the grave from a place where decay prevails to a sacred place. So now a believer lies in the grave and sleeps the sleep of death, and not many Christians have any inkling how much damage this attitude (which idolizes death as holy and splendid) has brought for God and his kingdom.

Where Redemption Is Found

INSTEAD OF LOOKING TO CHRIST, the one who rose from the dead (and whose grave no one gave a second thought), people started to look to *death* [for redemption]. To be sure, when cruel death snatches a loved one away people cannot hold back their tears of grief in spite of all their Christian faith. To be sure, millions of people break into heart-wrenching wails when grim death drags old and young into darkness. But the strength to counter death with eternal life was spent. Gone was the impulse for life that could lead toward a wisdom which thwarts death as much as possible even in our normal physical life. On the one hand people don't want to die, yet on the other hand they stagger toward death both figuratively and literally drunk. People who through their own fault have been sucked into the darkness of death comfort themselves with the idea that at the grave *death* will bring "redemption" to them.

In light of this situation, in which most of the world bows to the inevitable (as they see it), it is all the more difficult to defend the kingdom of God and the resurrection of life. Another harmful idea that has become generally accepted is that a person will be saved and fully satisfied through death *without* resurrection. It has gotten so bad that you can hardly touch on this subject without arousing touchy and resentful feelings. People fight for death like they fight for their own lives because they think salvation (meaning the fulfillment of their desire for happiness) is linked to death. I am very sorry to say that I have lost many friends in far-reaching circles since I seriously researched and zealously witnessed to the fact that we are justified in holding on to Christ while we are on this earth – to a Christ who is not to be equated with death and who does not promise salvation in the darkness of death but in the *abolition* of death.

The Bible is full of this hope. Wherever God reveals himself, eternal life shines forth on earth: already in Paradise; then at the time of Noah, when God made a covenant with the earth; at the time of Abraham, when God made a covenant for the benefit of all nations; at the time of Moses, with whom God made a new covenant for a new land, where streams of blessing and life were to flow if the people would understand [and obey] the guidelines of truth; at the time of the prophets, in the midst of terrible misfortunes for God's people, in the midst of sin's anguish and death's misery. Every figure who brought forth fruit for God on earth gave witness to the Creator's power for life in the body and on earth. If we remove these forerunners of resurrection and of life from the testimony of scripture, and if we separate the apostles and prophets from the life-giving miracles of God Almighty (miracles that foreshadow the kingdom of God, in which there will be no death), then we might as well put the Holy Bible on a shelf with other books and ask ourselves if we still want to read it. This is what we have come to. Who looks for answers in the Bible anymore? Most people are content as long as the Bible serves to uphold the viewpoints and traditions that have been passed down to them – for which they subscribe to the most contrived interpretations. Beyond that, no one is interested in scripture. People are satisfied with a religion that promises help against sin, death, and the devil when they die, but meanwhile sin, death, and the devil are free to rule as they have since time immemorial, and no one cares. And because no one can figure out how to square this with what shines out from Christ, and from the prophets and the apostles, anything reported [in the Bible] about eternal life and its appearance on earth (any example of death being abolished in the kingdom of God) is either dismissed as a fable or subjected to contrived exegesis to pacify our consciences. We act just like someone once said, "We who have the *church* do not need the remarkable results that the spirit of God can bring about in our bodies and in our lives as recorded in scripture."[2]

Foundation Stones for the New Creation

YET THE FIRE of the living God continues to burn in secret. Even though they are coated with the dust of death, there are secret supporters of life in Jesus who walk among us unnoticed and rejected. However, they have been solid in their testimony to life throughout the centuries. The thread of life and resurrection that proceeds from Christ, the risen one, had to go underground because it could not be connected to the masses in present-day Christianity. Still, this thread has come down to us. It did not get broken. Christ – he who is, and was, and is to come (Rev. 1:4, 8) – died in order to deliver God's creation and the masses. In the masses, no one can find the strength anymore to believe in Christ's great beginning of the new creation, let alone summon up the strength to actually join this new creation with body and soul. Nonetheless Jesus does live, and he does raise up his witnesses. We praise God that from the beginning we were drawn with irresistible force to the victor. This victor wants to grant us salvation in a heaven that is physically present to us. But even more than that, he has the power and authority to save us, which means that his life is revealed in us and his life overcomes death. This victor saves us through a new creation, which begins within us and in the light of which no death, no sorrow, and no weeping has any power even today (Isa. 25:8; Rev. 7:17, 21:4).

This very thing came to my father in his experiences, and we experienced it too, just at the moment when we thought we would choke to death in the dust of death.

---

2 For example, the distinguished biblical theologian Hermann Cremer opposed Christoph Blumhardt's hope, not explicitly but indirectly, in his book *Die Fortdauer der Geistesgaben in der Kirche* (Gütersloh: Bertelsmann, 1890).

But the glory of Jesus Christ proves itself in the wretched and poor who place their hope in nothing other than the revelation of the Word of life. In spite of their current battles against the flesh, they are allowed even today to see with their own eyes, to hear with their own ears, and to touch with their own hands (1 John 1:1–3) what Jesus is all about – Jesus who not only has the victory but also is alive. They look away from death. For them death no longer represents the bridge into eternal life. Death is of no account for those who die in order that Jesus may live. They do not reassure themselves with the hope that some fine day God will deliver them through *death*. They know that even today death will wreak havoc in their mortal bodies if they are not found in Christ. They do not need to wait for their dying moments to recognize death as an enemy.

They try to honor God and to bear fruit for God's kingdom by surrendering themselves to the blood of Jesus Christ. This could be called a dying for life. For if this blood, this death of Christ, is within us, it brings about liberation from death. We do not need to wait until after death to be saved. Anyways, we are not saved and blessed for our own sakes. We are saved and blessed when we know that God in Christ, the risen one, is receiving the honor due him in the lives of all those who reject anything to do with the flesh and death, no matter how tempting. These people press on toward the goal to win the prize (Phil 3:14). The prize will one day be revealed to the whole world as the new creation.

There would have been no point in Christ entering into human history and human flesh if in the end we have to give up on account of an irrevocable "law of death" (Rom. 8:2). Now that Christ has risen from the dead, and the prospect of death being overcome is in view, do you really want to say that Genesis 2:17, "You shall surely die!" is an irrevocable law? That would annul the Word of life in creation! Granted, for anyone squeezing himself into a deadly existence – bound by darkness and his carnal flesh – this law holds true. But Christ is exalted far above the history of all flesh. Those who reject the flesh, both in themselves and in their surroundings (no matter what form the temptations take) will be lifted up into eternal life even here on earth. Here on earth is where the last battle will be fought for the abolition of the *curse* of death.

When Death Creeps into Everything

THIS IS THE HOPE that shone in my father (though somewhat obscured by his time): he was absolutely certain that Jesus would appear soon, Jesus Christ, the risen one, the victor over all powers of darkness. We can go a step further to visualize this hope more clearly. The appearance of Jesus Christ, in and of itself, will not be enough to lift the blanket of death. We have to go hand in hand with Jesus by denying our flesh. This battle is not spared anyone who is looking forward to the abolition of death. It is remarkable, but the forces of death come to us looking like charming angels who wield the scepter over our whole being, body and soul. In this sense, maybe, those people are right who tip their hats to the "majesty of death," while it hardly ever occurs to them to stand in awe of the justice and truth of the majesty of God.

Without most people realizing it, the traditions of death have snuck into our human culture and have laid claim to us who are overcome by grief and despair. Then we cry out to God to save us. But we ourselves have opened wide every door in support of death. These charming, death-bringing customs infect our life at every rung, from the bottom to the top, from the physical life of the body to the mental activities of the soul. In the end even our spirit yields, giving up its defenses and letting itself be made into an advocate for inherently pernicious practices.

Death-bringing customs have crept into everything. This process starts with bad habits at the physical level, for example with the taste buds of people who eat and drink only what they like. It continues at the social level, where unreasonable demands are made on people so that they go to pieces before their natural time. It shows up in a mindset that makes people chase after external happiness and freedom. This mindset traps people by making them lust, body and soul, after the apparent necessities of a cultured life. Finally, this process ends with a confusing philosophy in which the more intellectual person winds up intoxicating himself in order to avoid feeling the realities of hardship. So we see that the traditions of death enter into everything and control our generation, whereas God should be the light of our lives.

Battling Death

NO ONE CAN START thinking about resurrection and life – and certainly no one can expect to see any fruits coming from Jesus Christ's resurrection – if they have not learned to distinguish at each of these levels in human life what comes from God and what comes from death. For some people (and sadly this is the case for many) God and death have merged into one point. And because death predominates, the God of life gets lost from sight. In this situation anyone who talks about the abolition of death will be laughed at.

But when death and God are seen to diverge and never to be united, then a light dawns on each stage of life. Beginning with the lowest level, the physical life, right up to the level of our highest spiritual impulses, this light divides between the claims of God and the demands of death, between the traditions of truth and righteousness (which are cradled in God's eternal creation) and the contemptuous habits of the flesh (which emerge from below). A battle ensues between these two, and this battle immediately makes demands on our whole life. This is where self-denial comes in. We have to turn away not only from stark habitual sin but also from aspects of life that are generally considered fine. In this way we can discern what is true and what is false. Even when what is false masquerades as an angel (2 Cor. 11:14) we can recognize it and reject it.

Of course, in this battle we will often be humiliated. We will have to ride out many a temporary standstill. We will often be misunderstood, and people will be annoyed at us. Things we all thought were good and holy will have to be smashed by the mighty blows of truth, since our physical sensations and our intellectual accomplishments are all entangled with sin.

This is most likely the reason why the whole world would rather turn down what could be achieved through the resurrection of Christ. Instead, they merely hope to get out of this mess at death. But anyone fighting for God's justice, his kingdom, and his life cannot accept this. They cannot settle for a faith that is dead since the works of God are not manifested in it (John 9:3–4, 14:12–14). The works of God cannot be given to a faith where there is no struggle – a faith that is merely the hope to be suddenly relocated to a happy life in heaven. Mind you, no one can even imagine what this happy life in heaven will be like until they have experienced a happy life [on earth] when body and soul are in harmony with God's justice and truth.

God's Lordship over All Creation

THEREFORE, WE DARE NOT wait only for the general abolition of death with the return of Jesus Christ. Rather, we are aware that we are called to join in the *work* for this salvation in fear and trembling (Phil. 2:12) and not grow weary in the race for this prize (1 Cor. 9:24). I earnestly dare to hope and ask God to restore the light that can finish off the deadly deception within us. I dare to look forward to the abolition of death in the hope that at the right moment we will be able to renounce whatever we recognize as leading to death. We dare this by preparing ourselves for any sacrifice and any change. I hope for God's almighty working and for the victory of justice given in Christ. Christ will not abandon us to our folly. Rather he will give us the insight to recognize the perfect virtues of him who has called us into his wonderful light (1 Pet. 2:9).

I dare to hope – but not for our own sakes. I look to Christ, the risen one, not because I want to shine in the eyes of others but for God's sake, for creation's sake. I turn my attention to this world – here, where the Creator said, let there be light in the darkness (Gen. 1:3) and where he created life; here, where he created man in the image of God, as son of the Most High, equipped with the breath of life and appointed to be God's representative for all living creatures (Gen. 1:26–28, 2:7, 2:15); here, where the Sabbath-rest for all living creatures beckons to us (Heb. 4:1, 9). As the indwelling of God in all forms of life that came from him, this [final] Sabbath beckons to us as the crowning of creation. Here on earth, where the Almighty works and moves, exalted above the unfolding of our sinful human race, we also see Jesus, the crucified and risen one. For the sake of God and his creation, we dare to put a spoke in the wheel of death's advance. We dare to raise our heads to honor God in his creation. This will give us the strength to persevere beyond the end of this world age – in which it almost seems as though the rattle of death were the signature of the living one. Zeal for God's honor, for justice, and for the life of God will equip us to carry on in this struggle in which our goal is the *abolition of death*.[3]

---

3 In the *Vertrauliche Blätter*, Christoph Blumhardt added this conclusion: "With these pages I close and say goodbye to my friends. Thank you for the patience you showed in listening to me. If some of what I wrote rocked your boat or even made you angry, I can't help it. I owed it to you to write what I knew to be true. I am convinced that many of you will have realized that I was not writing to cast a human discovery out into the world. I just want to witness to what I have experienced in my heart and know to be firmly grounded. I could have kept my mouth shut if I had wanted to please people. But for God's sake I had to speak up at least in an intimate circle. Many of my friends have turned their backs on me. They have forgotten that I have never sought to put myself forward. But many others will realize that I have sacrificed my life for the justice and truth of our God – and will continue to do so. His kingdom stands eternally. No matter in which way it comes, it will gain the victory, and here on earth all nations will see the salvation of God.

"At this point I do not know whether or not I will be able to keep in touch with friends by publishing any more of these newsletters. But I hope to find ways to stay in touch and I know that there is a connection uniting all those who love the Lord Jesus and who seek for the kingdom of God."

Afterword

Wolfgang J. Bittner

Blumhardt's Purpose

THE BOOK BEGAN as a conversation with friends about God's leading. What did God want to accomplish during his father's lifetime? How much of what was important in his time is still valid today? What does the living God want to change today? Because Blumhardt's thinking was deeply rooted in the Bible, he was convinced that in the kingdom of God times differ and times change. What was valid yesterday might be different today. God's instructions are not [always] timeless. At every hour and for every stretch of the way, we have to receive his instructions anew. The father was entrusted with a battle against darkness, which he fought to the end in the name of God. At that time the slogan God gave him was: "Jesus is victor in the battle against darkness and superstition." This also gave him the goal that God wanted him to achieve during that time – the apex of darkness and superstition was to be crushed so that God's victory could be enforced. God accomplished this goal to a great extent through the elder Blumhardt. The son recognized this as an act of God. That Jesus is victor is the solid foundation on which he also stands.

But why the changes? Because God keeps moving forward and expects different things from us now. This was Blumhardt's answer. What his father accomplished was not the goal, it was only a station on the way – a station on the path that God plans to take with his own. God did not stop at this station. Whoever wants to accompany God can't look back wistfully! He must carry on with determination. This idea was basic to Blumhardt's biblical understanding of God: God travels down a path in history. Faith means accompanying the living God on his path. Anyone who stands still is in danger of losing God. What was valid yesterday may be outdated today. As Blumhardt says, today we live in a new chapter of history, in which we have received a new assignment from God: "Die! For only then can Jesus live!"

We have not forgotten that Jesus is victor over all dark powers. We are well aware of the power of hidden forces. We know of the lingering inner bondages that still obstruct God's kingdom. But experiences in our day permit us to pay less attention to this. God has opened our eyes so we can see that it is our human selfishness that is resisting God – the selfishness called the flesh. If we can do away with this resistance, it will have even more important consequences than a victory over demons.

Therefore, in our day, we have to die, so that Jesus can live. This means that we want to be dead to whatever is human and to whatever focuses on people. Our human nature is not to be nurtured through God, through Christ, and through the Spirit – on the contrary, our human nature, our flesh, is to be revealed and judged through God, through Christ, and through the Spirit.

However, Blumhardt does repeatedly look back in this book – back into the Bible and back into the times of his father. What for? When we look back into the past, it sharpens our sight so we can see the vast hope that God has given in his promises. It also helps us to see human mistakes that we should avoid. Blumhardt, as far as it was revealed to him, pinpointed and condemned certain actions and courtesies of his father: too much deference for people, for church leadership, and for the pious self-indulgence of those who gathered around him. Blumhardt looked back only because he knew the unity between him and his father in the history of God was unshakable. When we look back into the past, it must never be to re-establish a former state of affairs. Our aim has to be only to hear more clearly the voice of God for today and to comprehend more fully God's goals for tomorrow. The son did not separate himself from his father. However, he continued with God further on the path that God had shown them in their common experiences. This is why the son now finds himself at a different place. For those who did not understand this and thought the previous station was the goal and stayed there, it seemed like the son was separating himself from his father.

Actually, Blumhardt's basic concern here is relevant to all times. How often do people try to find formulas or basic patterns in the Bible and in history under the slogan of finding "biblical" teachings? These formulas are supposedly valid for all time and are applied independently of God's will in history. Even today people are looking for "biblical directives." They think the Bible has directives for our human activities. They think all we have to do is discover these directives and then follow them accurately and faithfully enough so that God will answer according to the model he himself has set down. They think God has to act according to rules that apply equally for all times. They think he responds to our actions according to precise, fixed rules. But that is not so. God does not act simply according to what we do. He acts according to the path he is taking through history.

We must study the Bible again to find God's point of view for us today. Of course, there are basic rules for our actions, plans, and prayers. The church always has the responsibility of discerning God's will. But she must always include in the process the question of God's history: What do you, God, expect of me today, of your church, of your world? Next to the question of what are God's commands for our actions, we must add the question of what are God's decisions for history. It is not enough to know what God wants. We also have to know what God wants today. Merely to refer to scripture passages or to what God has done in times past is not enough.

We can learn a lot from Blumhardt on the topic of guidance. Blumhardt valued the Bible as the permanent source for discovering God. He learned from it and always told others to listen to and obey the scriptures. He learned from it how God acted in times past. He learned how God made his way through history. We can see basic truths, which sharpen our eyes and hearts so we can perceive God's voice more and more clearly today. A few examples:

> If you are chosen, it means you will be commissioned with a task and your life will become more intense. It does not mean that you are privileged.

> God's patience with his people does have an end.

> There are times when he is patient, but there are also times when he judges.

> The faith of one individual person can open the way for an entire nation.

> On the other hand, the faithlessness of a nation or a congregation can inhibit the faith of an individual or even stifle it entirely.

> God takes individual people with him on his way if they put themselves totally at his disposal.

> The path to life which God gives us goes through total surrender and through dying to our self-will, not around them.

God's demonstrations of power have to lead us to lay down any quest for ourselves, otherwise they will deteriorate.

In the end, Blumhardt aligned his hopes for the future according to the promises in scripture. He expected whatever God had promised in scripture to happen. Not more, but certainly not less!

In addition to taking the Bible seriously, Blumhardt could intuitively see the inner truth in human and historical events, which he took seriously too. He was not easily deceived by outward show. Long before the First World War he foresaw with trembling how things were developing and called it a judgment of God. Judgment did indeed come over Germany and Europe. Incidentally, this view was very different from that of other well-recognized church leaders of his time. He measured history against the Bible and realized that the arrogance of a nation and its rulers indicated the last stage before the fall. In his opinion, in order to understand the Bible we absolutely must have an unprejudiced mind and an unbiased historical view.

A third element for discerning God's will was at least as important to him, which clearly emerges in this book: to pay attention to the living guidance given to people in their daily lives and through experiences in which they find themselves. He called this listening to the "happenings" and "experiences" of God. In fact, at times when such guidance seemed abundantly clear, he even spoke of it as a "revelation." A person (or congregation) may well pray and read the Bible, but if they are not aware of God in their daily lives and the events around them, Blumhardt considered such a person (or congregation) not only to have taken an enormous step backward, but also to be terribly deaf. Instead, we should change our views according to what we have experienced. For this is how God guides his children on earth: he gives us tangible experiences of judgment and of grace – experiences which it would be a crime to pass over indifferently just to stay true to our old ways of thinking.

The movement in the elder Blumhardt's time received power and direction from concrete experiences of God, and so did the son. His experiences came from the same Spirit as in earlier times. But this same Spirit gives new experiences of God and new insights again and again. Blumhardt listened carefully for promptings of the Spirit in daily life and current affairs.

If we stand still, we will get separated from the living testimonies of God, which are hammering on the doors of our world today. Blumhardt's basic concern is that we should view the goals we think we have reached merely as stations on God's way; that we realize we can continue today to go with God on his way; and that we align our lives with the goals that God sets for himself for tomorrow. This whole book evolved along these lines. This is its core idea. Some of Blumhardt's ideas may apply only to his time. Some ideas may have been concealed from Blumhardt due to his position in history. But the way Blumhardt raises questions – asking what hindered the movement in his father's time from advancing, what hinders God's progress today, and how we might take hold of the goals that God has in mind for our world – shows an exceptional astuteness and prophetic clarity. Anyone who is looking for renewal of the church should consider this basic concern and Blumhardt's concrete suggestions for implementing it.

Thoughts about the Kingdom of God

WHEN BLUMHARDT WROTE this book, he was not writing a doctrine of history. He was trying to state his position and explain it to his friends – who were opposing him and criticizing him more and more sharply. Some even turned away from him. By clearly stating his position, he wanted to gain strength for the future. But what came to him during the process of writing (which for him remained connected to his controversy at that time) can be understood by us as a picture of how God uses people to make progress in history.

I would like to briefly outline this picture here, without claiming that it is either complete or well-balanced.

We should see history as a succession of different times. The changeover from one time to another takes place through a powerful upheaval that creates the new state of affairs.

God gives each time its own specific goal. What was valid during one time cannot simply be transferred to another. Times are stations. But God moves on.

God's progress in history is achieved through battles that God calls us to and that have to be won in his strength. But progress depends on whether God finds warriors who put themselves completely at his disposal for his goals and his hopes. These warriors have to become free of themselves and independent of their time. These are the people God uses to create his history.

God's battles are always fought on two fronts. One front is against resistance to God's kingdom that comes from without – from the circumstances of the time or from dark spiritual powers. But the other front lies within the people who walk with God and therefore within the church itself. Whoever wants to follow God and conquer has to surrender himself, his own will, to God – Blumhardt uses the biblical term his "flesh." When we die to ourselves, then Jesus can live in us. This is the battle that Blumhardt took on, and this is the front to which he tried to rally his friends. Most of them refused.

The decisive criterion for shaping the present is whether we can clearly and unflinchingly put love to God above love to our neighbor.

The course of history and true progress is above and beyond human intervention. For this reason Blumhardt perceived history as an ongoing work of God through the Holy Spirit. If you look at history through God's eyes, you will of course notice human activity and human failure, but above and beyond that you will be able to see a succession of God's creative deeds. It is not a question of men and women doing what they can with the available means. God himself must create within them the new life that he is looking for. And he will continue to do so. This is why Blumhardt thought of the Holy Spirit primarily as a creative spirit and this idea channeled his understanding of history. History, God's creative deeds, and the Holy Spirit belong together.

To live under God in the present we have to keep our eyes fixed on God's future. That is why we have to take God's promises and turn them into the hopes by which we lead our lives. If we look resolutely at these hopes and live according to them, then the future that God wants to bring about starts to take shape in our lives – the future that is often still veiled to us is given form in the present.

Three different hopes emerge, each essential in its own way for the shaping of history. First, we have all reason to hope for the Holy Spirit to come to us in greater measure than has been given so far. His coming will bring a time of judgment for the church and through that also a time of new creation. When we hope and pray for something new and lasting in history, it has to be given through the work of the Holy Spirit.

Second, in addition to the Holy Spirit, which God uses to create his history in and through people, God uses Zion, the place through which he works in the world. Blumhardt uses the biblical term "Zion" for a group of people who truly are a people of God because they do not live for themselves anymore. Through the Holy Spirit in Jesus Christ they place themselves totally at the disposal of the Father. Through the Holy Spirit, God wants to live within them, as in a little flock. They receive God's kingdom, so that they can be a place of refuge for all people and all nations.

Third, to this belongs the final goal for this earth, which God has predetermined: the abolition of death. God is not otherworldly. He does not draw us and our hopes away from this world. When we fix our hopes on God's promises, God is drawn into this world. Just because we know that any true progress is not our own doing, but can only be brought about by God creating something new through the Holy Spirit, our hope is the real hope for this world.

The Blumhardt Source Series

Johann Christoph Blumhardt
A Biography
Friedrich Zündel

The Gospel of God's Reign
Living for the Kingdom of God
Christoph Friedrich Blumhardt

Gospel Sermons
On Faith, the Holy Spirit, and the Coming Kingdom
Johann Christoph Blumhardt

Make Way for the Spirit
My Father's Battle and Mine
Christoph Friedrich Blumhardt

Printed in the USA
CPSIA information can be obtained
at www.ICGtesting.com
JSHW022342140824
68134JS00019B/1635